Cheers for *The Home*

"Working at home is more than a work option–it's a *lifestyle*. In *The Home Team: How Couples Can Make a Life and a Living by Working at Home*, Scott and Shirley Gregory equip couples with all the practical guidance and light-hearted humor they'll need to make this work-life option a *home run*."
  –**Lisa M. Roberts**, author of *How to Raise a Family and a Career Under One Roof: A Parent's Guide to Home Business*

"Blend current reality with age-old romanticism; add a pinch of flexibility, a dash of pragmatism and a scoop of humor. What have you got? *The Home Team: How Couples Can Make a Life and a Living by Working at Home*. What a wonderful gift the Gregorys give contemporary couples. This is an easy read and a thorough, well-organized treatment of an increasingly important topic."
  –**Paulette Ensign**, president, National Association of Professional Organizers, and author of *110 Ideas for Organizing Your Business Life*

"As part of a Home Team, I appreciated the Gregorys' emphasis on teamwork, as well as their willingness to go candidly into the challenges as well as the rewards, and their light, easy-to-read style of writing. From our own experiences, the issues they brought up are very real. I found myself feeling encouraged after reading it, knowing we are not alone in the all-too-real issues my husband and I face in our home business."
  –**Patti Taylor**, author of *The Enchantment of Opposites: How to Create Great Relationships*

"Scott and Shirley's enthusiasm for the at-home work life is contagious! This book will not only make you anxious to move your work home, but will humorously remind you of the pitfalls you may face, and gently instruct you about ways to avoid them. Whether or not working together is on your immediate agenda, this is a great book for all couples to read and discuss."
—**Jan Zobel**, author of *Minding Her Own Business: The Self-Employed Woman's Guide to Taxes and Recordkeeping*

"*The Home Team* is a thorough and engaging look at the work-at-home world–full of great advice and ideas, whether you're just thinking about it or you've been doing it for years."
—**Sue Robishaw**, artist, work-at-home partner, and author of *Homesteading Adventures: A Guide for Doers and Dreamers*

"This book is great in outlining the advantages a couple has in choosing to work at home together and provides tips to avoid the potential pitfalls. With the information given in this book, couples can learn to work and play together!!!"
—**Dr. Jon Kardatzke, M.D.**, marriage seminar leader and author of *Marriage Can Be Fun*

"Working with your spouse is both rewarding and challenging. *The Home Team* is the perfect coach for any couple who wants to be effective and successful in this endeavor."
—**David LeClaire**, author of *Bridges to a Passionate Partnership*

"If you're thinking of starting a home-based business with your life partner, reading Scott and Shirley Gregory's book, *The Home Team: How Couples Can Make a Life and a Living by Working at Home* is a *must!* This book covers every aspect of working together at home, from getting started to establishing goals, being productive, and personality conflicts.

"The Gregorys provide fascinating, in-depth glimpses into many successful home-based business couples' lives. These couples share their own creative solutions for getting along, communication, parenting, how to get away from it all and the true meaning of partnership. This is a book about love and passion–it's also about reality. It's about living and working together at home and the tremendous benefits of doing so. Best of all, the Home Team has the opportunity to develop a level of intimacy most couples only yearn to have in their lives.

"If you want more out of life and are considering the work-at-home wave, yet have questions and concerns, you'll find all the answers here! The Home Team lifestyle offers flexibility and tons of advantages. If you've been hesitating about starting that home business, these pages will fill you with inspiration and hope. You can have it all!"

–**Darla Sims**, author of *MAKING $$$ AT HOME: Over 1,000 Editors Who Want Your Ideas, Know-How & Experience*

"It's not easy writing a book about work, life, love and marriage, but Scott and Shirley Gregory have done it and hit each nail right on the head. Their book is alive with examples, humor, honesty and encouragement. I'd put it on the required reading list for couples who want to love and work together happily ever after."

–**Jay Conrad Levinson**, author of *Guerrilla Marketing* series

"Always useful, often playful. I wish I could have read it before my wife and I went into business. But after ten years together in the business, there still is much that we could take away and use."

–**Shel Horowitz**, author of *Marketing Without Megabucks: How to Sell Anything on a Shoestring*, and co-director, Accurate Writing & More, Northampton, Massachusetts

"The Gregorys' insight into the complex husband-wife/business partner relationship causes us to think about that part of our life, which is easy to ignore when you are wrapped up in business. We are now more aware about how our business partnering affects our marriage. ... Every couple who dreams about working together in a home-based business should read this book to get a jump-start on the relationship side of a husband-wife home business team."

–**John and Judy Coker**, owners, Broken Heart Publishing

"If you work at home as a couple, or think you may in the future, *The Home Team* is a must-read! You'll find so much to implement and you'll enjoy reading it!"

–**Marlene B. Brown**, author of *TechnoTouch: Managing Change for 21st Century Leadership of Self and Others*

"*The Home Team* is an invaluable resource for anybody who is operating or contemplating a home-based business. Sally and I have been implementing many of these concepts in our business with the results that our business is becoming more effective, and our home life more harmonious."

–**Joe Tye**, speaker and author of *Never Fear, Never Quit: A Story of Courage and Perseverance*

The Home Team

How Couples Can Make a Life and a Living by Working at Home

Scott Gregory

Shirley Siluk Gregory

Published by:
Panda Publishing
P.O. Box 3834
Naperville, IL 60567-3834
http://www.bookhome.com

Published by:
Panda Publishing
P.O. Box 3834
Naperville, IL 60567-3834
http://www.bookhome.com

Copyright © 1997 by Scott Gregory, Shirley Siluk Gregory
First Printing 1997
Printed in the United States of America

All rights reserved. No part of this book may be reproduced or transmitted in any form or by any means, electronic or mechanical, including photocopying, recording or by any information storage and retrieval system without written permission from the author, except for the inclusion of brief quotations in a review. Requests for permission should be made in writing to Panda Publishing.

"The Home Team" work-at-home books, newsletters, seminars and merchandise, as well as the plate and home logos, are trademarks of Scott and Shirley Gregory. Used with permission. All other brand names and product names used in this book are trademarks, registered trademarks, or trade names of their respective holders.

Publisher's Cataloging-in-Publication

Gregory, Scott A.
    The home team: how couples can make a life and a living by working at home / by Scott Gregory, Shirley Siluk Gregory.
    p. cm.
    Includes bibliographical references and index.
    Preassigned LCCN: 96-92429
    ISBN: 1-889438-32-4

    1. Home-based businesses.   I. Gregory, Shirley. II. Title.
HD2333.G74 1997   658'.041
                                  QBI97-40495

This book is dedicated to ...

*Marianne and Michael
Virginia and George*

*... living examples of the value of teamwork in marriage,
whether the times are peaceful or challenging.*

Contents

Acknowledgments	13
Introduction	17
Chapter 1: The We Generation	23
Chapter 2: Score Another Two Touchdowns for the Home Team: Fourteen More Reasons to Love the Lifestyle	45
Chapter 3: Home Team Fundamentals	64
Chapter 4: Your Relationship: Roles, Goals and Understanding	90
Chapter 5: Slobs vs. Neat Freaks (and Other Challenges)	112
Chapter 6: Mom and Dad Day Care Inc.: How to Stay Productive While Enjoying the Wonders of Work-at-Home Parenting	136
Chapter 7: Getting Away From It All When It's All at Home	154
Chapter 8: Fooling Around at the Office: How to Ignite and Maintain Passion When You Work at Home	173
Chapter 9: Home Team Women: As Close as You Can Get to Having It All	195
Chapter 10: The Home Boys: Men at Work–and Play–in the Home	212
Chapter 11: Root, Root, Root for the Home Team	230
Afterword	241
Recommended Reading	244
Index	248

"Life has taught us that love does not consist in gazing at each other but in looking together in the same direction."
 —*Antoine de Saint-Exupery*

Disclaimer

This book is designed to provide information in regard to the subject matter covered. It is sold with the understanding that the publisher and authors are not engaged in rendering legal, accounting, marital, or other professional services. If assistance in these areas is required, the services of a competent professional should be sought.

It is not the purpose of this book to reprint all the information that is otherwise available to the public, but to complement, amplify and supplement other texts. Readers are urged to read all the available material, learn as much as possible about running a home business and having a successful marriage relationship, and tailor the information to individual needs. Anyone who decides to work at home should expect to invest plenty of time and effort, not get rich quick. But many couples have found that home businesses, as well as working together, are the most satisfying ways to live and work.

Every effort has been made to make this book as complete and accurate as possible. However, there may be mistakes, both typographical and in content. Therefore, this book should be used only as a general guide and not as the sole source of work-at-home and marital information.

The individuals and businesses named in this book are to provide insight into the work-at-home life. They might not endorse any or all aspects of this book, nor should their mention constitute endorsements of their products and services.

The purpose of this book is to educate, inspire and entertain. The authors and Panda Publishing shall have neither liability nor responsibility to any person or entity with respect to any loss or damage caused, or alleged to be caused, directly or indirectly, by the information contained in this book.

If you do not wish to be bound by the above, you may return this book to the publisher for a full refund.

Acknowledgments

We begin with a standing ovation for the couples who took time out of their busy Home Team schedules to be interviewed for this book. The openness, honesty and sincerity they showed us was humbling, to say the least. This book would not have been as complete without their input, and certainly would not have been as enjoyable to write without their on-the-record anecdotes and quotes.

We told them we wanted the full story–good and bad–about the work-at-home arrangement, and gave them all the option of keeping part or all of the conversations as background. Not one of them ever said, "Don't print that," even though we touched on some of the most personal aspects of married life. Whether their names appear again in the following pages, their input was vital and appreciated.

Among these couples are: Richard Adin and Carolyn Edlund, John and Gail Baker, Jeff and Liz Ball, Brad and Rosemarie Barbeau, Dan and Maureen Carlson, Alex and Meera Censor, Richard and Jodi Creager, Jeeni Criscenzo and Joe, Michael and Marjorie Desgrosseilliers, Mark and Susan Detwiler, Julie Dorfman and Jerry Herst, Eric and Jean Flaxenburg, Ronald Lee Fleming and Renata von Tscharner, Jerry and Susan Fletcher, Jim and Michelle Foy, Carlos and Sherian Frey, Ham and Ellie Hamilton, Bob and Margaret Hanson, Ed and Colette Hoover, Jeff Justice and Diane Pfeifer Justice, Carol Kurtz and Steve Mudd, Jerry and Colleen Larson, Keith and Jo Lutnes, Bill and Eloise McGraw, Toby Myles and James Patterson, Steve and Vicki Palmquist, Bob and Charlene Pettingell, Valerie Saint-Gaudens and Kenne Swink, Terry and Susan Schandel, Bob and Carolyn Sherman, Aron and Simcha Shtull-Trauring, Robert Timothy Wickes and Nina Tinsley-Wickes.

We had the fortune to meet many of these couples thanks to the help of people at various groups and associations, including Beverly Williams, president and founder of the American Association of Home-Based Businesses; Neal Lubow of the Association of Home Businesses; the folks at Buy Idaho, and the San Diego Home Business Association; Ronald Brill of the Independent Worker's Association; Marcia Stuckey of The Nebraska Development Network, and Julie Schopick at the Mount Prospect (Illinois) Chamber of Commerce. Regards also to Thalia Poulos, who provided us with plenty of tips that will make our lives more organized.

Thanks to Steve Michals, who puts together knockout exhibits at Prairie Display in Elmhurst, Illinois, and is an amazing entrepreneur in his own right. And to Sue and Dan Michals, Sue Turai, Lisa Turai, Shirlee and the Jims LeBrun, as well as the Garys, Bea and Tyler Gregory.

We owe plenty of gratitude to Dr. Robert Barnes, who is helping kids and families daily at Sheridan House in Ft. Lauderdale, Florida; Jay Conrad Levinson, a true marketing guerrilla; and fellow work-at-home author Lisa Roberts for their contributions in making *The Home Team*™ newsletter even more valuable to subscribers.

Steve Lundy, a former work pal, shared his time and talents to make some photographic contributions to this book and our marketing endeavors.

Gabriele Massie, Darla Sims and Jan Zobel, writers of fine work-at-home and business books, broke away from their writing and businesses to look over our manuscript. So did authors Joe Tye, an inspiration to many entrepreneurs, and Dr. Jon Kardatzke, who has taught many that marriage can be fun.

The decade started with the Florida connection. Jim Barentine and Glen Woodfin are friends who encouraged Scott and taught him plenty about good business and people. Those two, along with Bubba and Sandy Pratt, Tim and Connie Foley, and many of their business associates, instilled the entrepreneurial spirit deeper inside of us.

Another entrepreneur, Paul Traverso, stopped filling news holes a few years ago in favor of filling stomachs at Traverso's Restaurant in Naperville, Illinois. His frank review of our book made us consider some important questions. Paul and his brother, Mike, truly exemplify what the restaurant business should be.

Dr. Wade Horn provided us with a lengthy interview as well as forwarded plenty of research that aided in the men's chapter. His work on behalf of fathers is something this world desperately needs.

Michael Larsen gave us input and encouragement on this project in its early stages many, many years ago.

Thanks to Dan Jones, our favorite hockey partner and attorney, and Mike Stotz, who has been a friend since Scott put his first crayon to paper. Thanks also to Liz Voss, a determined writer and stay-at-home mom, and to Donna Wallace for their longtime friendship.

We have learned a great deal about this business from many fine participants of the Publishers Marketing Association listserv. From this list, Shel Horowitz, Paulette Ensign, Marlene Brown, David LeClaire, Sue Robishaw, John Coker, Patricia Taylor, Michelle Lambing and Nadine MacLane graciously shared their thoughts about our manuscript.

Thank you to Gary and Mary Lynn Leland, Kent and Patti Nelson, Steve and Kathy Gasser, and Randy and Jenny Mittelstaedt, a small group of fine people, for their friendships, Friday nights and beyond.

To the five members of the Zoo Crew–it's play time.

Most of all, thanks to God, for allowing us to find each other, for our talents, and for giving us the strength and determination to overcome many obstacles on our way to bringing you this book. Both the end product and our lives are better for it.

Introduction

After a typical twelve-hour, stress-filled workday at the daily newspaper where we used to work in suburban Chicago, we headed down the road from our office to an all-night restaurant to decompress over a few (dozen) coffees.

It was a date early in our relationship. We met at work and developed a friendship for about five months before we began dating. Of course, our closest friends and some colleagues advised against it: "Don't go out with someone you work with–it will only lead to trouble," was a common comment, usually unsolicited, both before and after the fact.

Not that dating someone at work was entirely comfortable at the start. We weren't sure how to act. We knew better than to paw each other in the workplace–which tends to make colleagues retch, and we feel the same when we see that–but what about the little things? Do we walk in together? Should we leave together? Do we tell anyone or everyone we are dating? We quickly decided not to care what anyone else thought–just do what we wanted and act like professionals. As time went on, we started to ask each other what all the fuss about dating an office colleague was about.

In fact, it was wonderful to have each other around most of the day to share the joys and frustrations of work. Our jobs–Shirley as a political reporter and Scott as an editor in a different department–were typical for newspapers: a lot of pressure-packed work for little pay. Bizarre work hours. In fact, if it weren't for the opportunity to date a colleague, our schedules would have left little time for a social life at all.

As the waitress poured our coffee, we began our date the usual way, by exchanging thoughts and laughs about the happenings of the workday. Post apple pie, the time seemed right to find out something deeper about each other. Scott asked Shirley a simple but pivotal question: "What would be the perfect way to live your life?"

Four words flowed from her lips without missing a beat: "Write books and freelance," she said, nodding with conviction.

Scott's jaw dropped. To the word, it was the same response he would have given had she posed the question to him.

Fast forward to May 1992. The newsroom was buzzing with excitement for weeks about news of impending changes at the paper. Had the company finally pried opened the checkbook to allow us to give better and wider-reaching coverage, as had been discussed? Would we finally switch to the modern page design?

When the news was delivered, it blindsided all of us, from the delivery drivers to the managing editor: the paper was changing format from daily to weekly, and our office was closing. We were all fired in a few weeks, although the company was kind enough to allow us all to reapply for lower-paying posts at the "new-and-improved" weekly paper.

The final weeks made us feel like death row inmates awaiting execution. Some colleagues dejectedly reapplied to the new paper right away; others prepared their resumes to

Introduction

go on to other jobs. We waited until the last minute, unsure of what to do and dreading taking a step backward at that point in our careers.

The night before the application deadline, we stood in our kitchen, forms in hand. Should we take the safe route, or was the time right for a bold move to self-employment? Despite all the terrifying uncertainties the future held, one after the other, we tore up the forms and slam-dunked them in the trash can. Our "Home Team" was formed.

But what to do next? Both of us being voracious readers of nonfiction, we went out and bought every book about working at home we could get our hands on. Many of those books gave fabulous advice on starting and operating home businesses, but something vital was missing. While a couple of authors touched on the subject, there wasn't a book that discussed at length the lifestyle benefits and challenges of running a business at home with your spouse.

Just as had been the case when we started dating at the office, the opinions began flowing in: "Don't start a business together. What if it doesn't work? What if you split up because of it? What if, what if, what if ... "

It didn't take long to discover that working this way could be a fabulous way to share our lives. In fact, we knew early on that it had the potential to be the perfect way. But it also presented challenges we didn't anticipate. Nor was there enough information out there to smooth those rough spots. How do we keep business from interfering with our home lives? What do we do when there are business disagreements that affect our relationship? Why did the house suddenly look as if the Tasmanian Devil had moved in, and what could we do about it?

Our first year of self-employment as freelance newspaper and magazine writers was successful, but we were still volleying ideas about our first book. In June 1993, we began researching the book we wished we could have purchased when we started working together. *The Home Team* is the realization of that quest.

Whether you are simply toying with the idea of working with your spouse, or you have been working together for decades, you will find plenty of useful information here. While *The Home Team* was written primarily for spouses who work for themselves in the home, much of the book also will aid those who work at home whose spouses work conventional jobs, and telecommuters.

We decided from the start it was imperative to provide you with information from a diversity of work-at-home experiences. Our book contains information gained from in-depth phone, in-person and e-mail interviews with Home Team couples worldwide from 1993 through 1997, as well as research into the subject.

The saying goes that the best experience is someone else's. We hope your businesses and relationships will benefit from what we, collectively, did right, and by avoiding the pitfalls we faced. Any work-at-home couple will tell you their special relationship isn't always easy. Nothing good in life is. But it can be more than worth it. It can be wonderful.

We thought it was important that you have the opportunity to meet most of the couples who shared their stories, rather than identify everyone anonymously. In only a few instances did we choose to omit names to protect identities. All couples we interviewed gave their permission to be quoted in the book, and we thank them again profusely for that opportunity. Their sharing attitude will make all our work-at-home lives better as a result.

While we have gone to great lengths to ensure timeliness, the nature of book publishing does not cooperate in that effort. People change, businesses open and close, and relationships evolve. Those we interviewed were talking from a perspective of a certain period in their lives, and that input was weaved into appropriate areas throughout the book. We

Introduction

ask that those quoted in the following chapters whose business or relationship situations change write us with the details if they feel the need, and we gladly will include those updates in subsequent editions of *The Home Team*.

It is important to do your homework before undertaking any business endeavor, and the purchase and reading of this book is a wonderful step in that effort. One thing we found out quickly after we started working for ourselves is, our education can never end. The further we go in life and business, the more there is to learn. *The Home Team* will focus primarily on showing you ways to make your special relationship more enjoyable and less stress-filled, which in turn can have a positive effect on your business. We urge you to read other books with more nuts and bolts about how to run businesses successfully, or even return to school for added studies, if necessary. Some of our favorite books are listed in the "Recommended Reading" at the end of this book. We believe it's equally important to read good books about improving your marital relationship. We hope you will make a commitment to reading and applying as much as you can about how to better both your businesses and your marriage.

We've committed our professional lives to helping, informing, inspiring and entertaining those who work at home. To help home-based business partners on an ongoing basis, we publish *The Home Team*™ newsletter. It elaborates on much of what is discussed in this book, as well as contains columns written by experts in their fields, including relationships, marketing and working with kids. You are entitled to a free copy as thanks for purchasing this book. Please turn to the back for details.

Now, please join us as we take a look at how to form a successful Home Team. If you have been working together for years, it might be tempting to skip the opening chapters. Please don't! There might be ideas you never thought of, or ones you have strayed from as the years have gone by. It never hurts to return to the fundamentals.

We'll begin by taking a look at this trend, and why forming a Home Team can be the ultimate way to live, love and work.

Scott Gregory
Shirley Siluk Gregory

Chapter 1

The We Generation

Each of us is having an affair with our business partner, and it's time we let you in on our secret.

The affairs take place right in our homes–often during business hours–day after day, month after month, year after year. And husbands and wives in the United States and throughout the world are joining in by the millions.

These married couples have decided to mix their love for each other with home-based businesses. They have said goodbye to the corporate team and hello to "The Home Team."

Side by side, these home-based entrepreneurial couples we call Home Teams are not only working to determine their professional and financial destinies, but also making commitments to share their lives in a special way.

Handled properly and lovingly, a Home Team not only can be a good way to live, it can be the perfect way for husbands and wives to share their lives. It's a chance to live an exciting, memorable, meaningful and satisfying life–together. A chance to spend more time with each other, more time with the kids, develop common goals and dreams, and reap the personal and monetary satisfaction of dual careers. A chance to reclaim control of your work and personal lives in today's out-of-control world.

This is a book about love, but also about reality. Building a good marriage isn't easy. Neither is running a successful business. Combining the two presents many personal, marital and professional challenges. Handle them poorly, and both the relationship and businesses will suffer. Handle them right, and you will be on your way to designing and living life under your terms.

Consider *The Home Team* your teammate in that quest. This book is a guide you can turn to time and time again throughout the years, as your relationship and businesses grow, and new opportunities and challenges arise. Whether you have worked at home together for decades or are toying with the idea, there is plenty here for you:

• If you work as a Home Team in the same or separate businesses, full or part time, we will provide you with plenty of ideas to help you get the most enjoyment out of working together. Do you ever face challenges with the unique mix of business and personal life? Would you enjoy more romance with your spouse? We will look at these and many other issues. Whether the arrangement is smooth or rocky, every Home Team can benefit from fine tuning.

• If you are a couple in traditional work situations–either both holding jobs, or as a single-earner and home-maker–who are looking for more out of life, *The Home Team* will show you the potential benefits of the arrangement, help you determine whether you are willing to commit to what it takes to work together, give you the information and courage to make the leap should you decide to proceed, and help keep you on the right track. You can learn from the experiences of ourselves and many other couples–from our joys and struggles—who have entered this workstyle before you;

• Women, if you are torn between making a mark in the business world and staying home with the kids, we will show you how to have it both ways;

• Men, you can be a solid financial provider and play a bigger role in the household, and in your kids' lives;

• If one of you is a solo home worker, we know you have seen the benefits of home-based work and hope to convince you that your lifestyle could be even better by bringing your spouse home, too.

When you form a Home Team, your house—whether a mansion or shack—provides a single venue for two people in love to combine all aspects of life.

Sports teams know the power of the home-court or home-field advantage. Put the Green Bay Packers in Lambeau Field, and it's a rare Sunday afternoon they don't head home victorious. Send them on the road to the Metrodome or the Meadowlands, however, and the Packers' advantage is diminished. It's not the building that makes the difference. It's the atmosphere—the support that can be found only at home.

You don't need seventy thousand screaming fans to egg you on every day. It's already hard enough getting quality time in the bathroom. But you can build that same feeling of support—working with *your* spouse in *your* arena under *your* terms—every day when you're part of a successful Home Team.

A marriage of two trends

Some couples you will meet in these pages started their home businesses in the 1970s, when the home worker wave was just a ripple. They are true pioneers of modern home work, having overcome the stigmas that were long attached to both running home businesses and working together. Today, though, the two trends they helped create are merging—the number of home businesses is skyrocketing, as is the number of "copreneurs," a term for modern-day entrepreneurial couples.

Renowned social observers—and collaborative couple—John Naisbitt and Patricia Aburdene say in their book *Megatrends for Women* that the future is now for couples working together in business: "The 1980s was the decade of the entrepreneur—individuals committed to a new vision of business outside the corporate hierarchy. The 1990s will be the decade of entrepreneurial couples."

A survey by Massachusetts Mutual Life Insurance Co. of Springfield, Massachusetts, shows that husband-wife teams now are the most common type of family-owned business.

Usually looking for financial independence, creative freedom or to be their own bosses, these couples decide to go into business for themselves. And where better for couples to set up shop than in the home? On the financial side, studies have shown that ninety-five percent of home businesses turn a profit in the first year. Compare that to a conventional small business failure rate exceeding fifty percent in the initial year and eighty to ninety percent over a decade.

While the financial odds favor home businesses, most home workers instead prefer to focus on improved quality of life. A survey by *Income Opportunities* magazine found that ninety-four percent of home business owners said they enjoy working from home most of the time. Sixty-three percent said they enjoy working from home *all* the time. Once removed from the rat race, many home workers say they wish they had escaped years earlier.

And few miss the commute. No more putting up with daily packed buses, trains and subways. No more sucking car exhaust on the expressway during the morning and afternoon standstills. Millions of Americans in traditional jobs will throw away a decade of their lives commuting, studies have shown.

Accountants, architects, consultants, mail-order entrepreneurs and thousands of other home-based professionals are saying they have better uses for that wasted time, thank you. IDC/Link, a New York-based research and consulting firm, found the number of full- and part-time home workers in the United States ballooned from twenty-six million to more than forty million between 1991 and 1996. This included about fifteen million full-time entrepreneurs, sixteen million part-time business owners and ten million telecommuters–employees of a company who do all or part of their work at home.

Although predictions vary significantly, most place the number of home workers in the United States between fifty million and seventy-five million in the year 2000, with growing numbers in a full-time capacity. The so-called "silent workforce" is starting to make some major noise.

The U.S. Government, certain that there must be more to all of this than the desire to work in one's underwear, has been increasingly curious about this trend. The Small Business Administration, eager to sort out the real from the hype about working at home, commissioned a report from Joanne Pratt, a consultant from Dallas. *Myths and Realities of Working at Home* stated that home-based work is good for the economy and worth encouraging, in most cases, for both men and women. Home workers gain both personal and financial benefits from the arrangement, she found.

Using data gathered from more than seventeen thousand people, the Pratt report aimed to answer the questions, "Does working at home make good business sense?" and "Are the individual and the family helped or harmed by working at home?" The study discovered that home-based businesses, in many instances, achieved results similar to conventional businesses: "The findings dispel the myth that income from home-based business activity is insignificant either to the economy or to individuals. With some exceptions, home-based business owners are surprisingly similar to non-homebased business owners in the income they earn and their patterns of work." The report found no significant negative effects on the family, but named some clear benefits. One is parental child care: "Only a business owner has enough control over a work schedule to make child care even a possibility."

Best of both worlds

Just as a good marriage allows a husband and wife to thrive on each others' strengths and compensate for weaknesses, the merging trends of copreneurship and home business–either of which alone can provide great benefits–into a Home Team creates tremendous potential.

Copreneurs who set up businesses away from home automatically separate their work and home life into two arenas. That's desirable only if they have no interest in having those overlap. They share the experience of working together, but miss out on the many benefits of working at home.

And, business ventures outside the home tend to be riskier. Investment and overhead typically are greater in a conventional business. Large numbers of employees present their own headaches and heartaches. With so much on the line, you might wait longer to enjoy the fruits of entrepreneurship, or stress yourself out with worries about whether the business will survive and you and your family will make it financially. It's a lot of risk for the pleasure of seeing your business name in neon.

Macaulay Culkin in: Home Alone 4

As for the solo home business, where one spouse works at home and the other holds a traditional job, a major drawback ensues: loneliness. In fact, in survey after survey, this turns up as the number one complaint of home workers. These couples don't see each other more than those who work in separate offices, and the spouse at home reports feeling isolated. No boss, which is great. But no human contact, either, which can be unhealthy over the long haul.

Although the phone and Internet can keep you in touch with others during the solo times, they can't match having someone you love at home with you.

Mental health professionals have found a high correlation between loneliness and stress. If you're breathing, you can find a million things to stress yourself out, and the belief that you're shipwrecked on a work-at-home island most days might head that stress list and take a major toll in the long run–even if you are a true believer in the home office lifestyle.

Add your spouse to the home businessplace and you have an office in not only the physical but mental sense. Even if you are swamped with work and can't see much of each other, it's amazing how reassuring it is to hear footsteps and a voice in another room. You also have someone to take a lunch break with, and complain to about the guy you just called for the twenty-third time who won't pay his bill.

If you are working at home by yourself, consider a greater vision: Why not share your home and work life with your spouse, and build businesses and chase dreams together?

Revisiting the past, with a modern twist

When we meet someone new and tell him or her that we work together at home, we frequently get the same response, "Oh, it's just like the old days. Just like a mom-

and-pop shop." While the locale is the same, the traditional mom-and-pop shop is a far cry from the business arrangement of most modern couples. Let's look at a hypothetical comparison:

Flip back the calendar to the 1930s, when the Smith family wants to take advantage of the American Dream by starting a home-based business. The family moves into a two-flat downtown and decides to live upstairs and set up a butcher's shop below.

It doesn't matter who is going to be working how much–when the sign goes up in the window, it's going to read, "Joe's Meats." He's going to call the shots and take credit for the bucks, but you can bet he's not going to let the rest of the family lie around upstairs and listen to Abbott and Costello on that mind-numbing radio all day.

Mom will keep track of the bookwork, and she and the kids will help take orders up front and package chops in the back. Mom will disappear upstairs at times during the day to prepare lunch, dinner, and bake a cherry pie for dessert. The shop closes at 5 p.m., cleanup by Dad and the kids takes a half hour and dinner is on the table at 5:35. Sharp.

Flash forward to today, and Joe's grandchild Mike is vice president-meat for a major supermarket chain. Mike's wife, Mary, is vice president-poultry for a competitor. The Smiths' combined income is darned impressive–and so is their Victorian home in the suburbs–but they don't see much of each other, and their two kids are beginning to call the snotty twentysomething at day care, "Mommy."

To make matters more unsettling, a new clothing-meat conglomerate, K-Meat, has swallowed a huge market share, and rumor has it cutbacks are imminent at the Smiths' companies.

Mike and Mary acknowledged years ago that meat and poultry aren't all they are cut out to be, and they have been talking forever about their dream of starting a consulting business from home. They finally decide that enough is enough, and take the entrepreneurial plunge.

Now, Mike and Mary both hold master's degrees and have worked their rump roasts off to get where they are. What would happen if Mike tells Mary he wants to follow his grandfather's business plan: Mike is credited with all the business glory, but they are going to share the work? And, by the way, to have dinner on the table every night at 5:35–sharp? If Mary doesn't drop dead of laughter, she'll certainly head out and look for a new job–and probably a new husband.

Stereotypical business roles are out for most home-based couples today. A Home Team might vary in business responsibilities and the amount of time they work, but the power is often shared, or at least distributed more equally than in the past. It's a workstyle that can give both partners a greater sense of pride and accomplishment in work life. And, as we will discover, the same holds true on the family side.

Where did all the time go?

In even the most loving and stable working families, the catch word today is sacrifice. In the 1950s, experts predicted we would all be sitting pretty at this point in time. Technology, the experts said, would enable us to do our jobs faster and more efficiently, and lop a day–maybe two–off our work week. At last, we would have that coveted extra time for ourselves and our families.

Instead, most husbands–and now wives, too–today find themselves on the treadmill even longer, thanks to technology and its bastard child, corporate downsizing. You can do your job quicker, but while you're at it, do more of it. Forty hours. Fifty hours. Sixty or more hours a week.

The Twenty-First Century is suddenly pounding on our front door, and no one is home. Those without jobs are screaming there aren't enough good ones. Others hate their work. Many who love what they do find they have time for little else. All know the phrase "job security" has become an oxymoron.

Most dual-income working couples say it's financial necessity–either to meet the requirements of life or maintain a lifestyle–that sends them both out the door to work every day. Many of these same couples complain they don't see enough of each other or their kids. In many cases, they also discover the two-income rat race still doesn't bring in enough money.

And what about the lifestyle of the single-earner, or that of the traditional entrepreneur, in which one spouse hauls in a hefty income but is practically a stranger to his or her family? Is that kind of arrangement any better?

In many cases, it's sacrifice without satisfaction.

Marriage in body and spirit

Arthur and Guinevere. Romeo and Juliet. Dr. Zhivago and Lara. Great literature and real-life history are crowded with stories of lovers wrenched apart for years–even a lifetime–by tragic circumstances. It makes for great romantic reading, but lousy life. Are most couples today better off? Too many people are spending the bulk of their lives apart from the ones they love the most.

Take, for example, a typical professional couple who commute to separate offices. To beat traffic and ensure themselves some quiet time before the phones start ringing, they have to be awake by 5 a.m. and out the door an hour later. They can't commute together because they work on opposite ends of town, and they often stay late at the office–both to catch up on an overwhelming workload and to sit out the worst of evening rush hour–so they usually don't see each other again until 7 p.m. or later. After dinner and taking care of household business—or, worse, a few more work projects left over from the office—it's almost time to get ready for bed. In all, they have had three or four non-sleeping hours together, most of which was spent scurrying around and showering, dressing, cooking or cleaning.

Other lives are even more complicated. Perhaps one couple has the same work routine, but two children on top of it all. Another couple with kids might work staggered hours to juggle child-care duties. In other cases, one or both spouses regularly take business trips. However you look at it, for five or six days a week over a period of thirty-five to forty-five years, most working couples are lucky to steal a couple of hours a day together out of twenty-four. That kind of time investment is better geared toward a hobby, not a marriage.

A typical husband and wife today love each other but end up caught in this vicious circle: they both are working jobs because they say they must, because they love their family and want to provide a good lifestyle. Then, as a result, they see little of each other or their kids. So they're working to make everyone happy, but no one's happy with the results of their work.

A husband and wife in love can make any work and marriage arrangement function if they are dedicated to making both a success. But when couples go about working at home properly, they don't have to choose between a career and a family—a decision some job-holders, traditional entrepreneurs and housewives have, consciously or subconsciously, felt obligated to make.

There are plenty of people in these categories who are thrilled with their work and family lives, and that's wonderful and admirable. We all should strive to live life in a way that's best for ourselves and our families. There are also couples who have worked together at home whose lives fell horribly out of kilter because of the way they handled the arrangement. The simple act of working together by no means guarantees a satisfying and successful life.

But when a couple commits to forming a Home Team–and takes the right steps to make the arrangement successful–they power up a combination that can't be beat.

Most Home Team couples we interviewed acknowledged that working at home allowed them to gain control of and enjoy more areas of their lives. Most said that, while they face plenty of struggles, they would go back to the typical work world only if finances forced them to, and they would be kicking and screaming all the way. The job world has a whole different look once you become work-at-home teammates.

Terry and Susan Schandel, accountants from Portland, Oregon, were married Nov. 29, 1969, but also celebrate another anniversary each year on Oct. 1. That was the date in 1978 they began working together from home as certified public accountants.

The Schandels say they had drifted apart throughout most of the 1970s. Their full-time jobs had kept them away from each other most of the time, and, as a result, they had little to talk about during the few hours they were together each night before bed. "It was our different job stresses," Terry says. "We had difficulty relating to each other–we didn't see each other."

In 1975, Terry began working from home and, in 1978, Susan joined him in business. Today, the Schandels talk about working from home as the rebirth of their marriage. They give equal weight to their wedding and work-at-home anniversaries each year. "We were married from six in the evening until six in the morning," Susan says. "In 1978, we also became married from six in the morning to six at night."

"Our work is enjoyable and fun now," Terry says. "Before, work was kind of drudgery. We have the opposite problem now of not knowing when to stop."

When you share so much more of the workday with the one you love, even work is more exciting.

Changing times: thank technology

Before we go cursing technology for its role in making the job world what it is today, we need to put our hands together and cheer its part in allowing more people to work at home.

A single pair of hands on the keyboard now can access information and complete jobs it once took tens or even hundreds to do. Computers and software, once the tool only of powerful corporations, are now available–and affordable–to the masses. And, thanks to the passage of time and simplification of many computer models, most of us have gotten over our fear of computers, or are at least making progress in therapy.

Add a fax machine, modem, and a few phone lines, and you can get in touch with just about anyone, anywhere. Why leave the home at times you neither want to or need to?

Ways Home Teams work together

We believe the ideal way for couples to share their lives is for them to be self-employed, building a business they enjoy together, and spending the bulk of their work days together at home. This arrangement offer the greatest chances for intimacy, understanding and common goals. It also allows the greatest flexibility for business, fun and child care.

But not all Home Teams want to follow this pattern. Couples can find happiness and success in an array of work-at-home situations. You should form a Home Team that best suits your wants, needs and talents.

We do hope, however, that your Home Team is more than simply two desks in the basement. Let's say a husband is in outside sales and his wife is a real estate agent. Both might run their businesses from home, but neither spends much time working there, and they don't see each other during the work day. In this case, it would be difficult to take advantage of many Home Team benefits.

Nobody in any home business stays home all the time, and, unless you're president of Boo Radley Enterprises, you wouldn't want to. But to be a true Home Team, you and your spouse need to spend a significant portion of workdays together under the same roof.

Remember, we're talking about forming a Home Team for reasons beyond money. Money is vital–you can't be a Home Team for long or continue to be one without enough of it coming in. As the saying goes, love doesn't pay the bills. But we're talking about making a life *and* a living.

Your businesses also might evolve over time. You might begin building a business as a part-time Home Team while you keep your "day jobs" and work toward entering your business full time. Or, you might decide to switch from running separate businesses to the same business. There are plenty of options, depending on your wants, needs and tolerance for risk.

How do Home Teams work? Although every arrangement differs depending on the types of businesses you decide to run, we will put them in what tends to be a descending order of potential lifestyle benefits:

- **They work together in business ventures.** Valerie Saint-Gaudens was fortunate. At nineteen, an age when most college kids are majoring in partying and clueless about their futures, she knew her destiny: she fell madly in love with jewelry making. "When I took my first jewelry class at nineteen, I went wild for it, and realized I could be creative and make a living at it," she says.

For a while, however, she thought that living would come through working for someone else. Her dreams turned to landing a job as an in-house designer for a major jewelry manufacturer. A company with financial and human resources would allow her to produce her designs without having to worry about the business details–or so she thought. However, a wage job left her without rights to royalties for her creative work, making her frustrated and miserable.

In 1985, fourteen years after that first jewelry class, her personal and professional life changed. She met Kenne Swink, a record promoter for a major music company, and she quit her job and began a business from home.

They were married in 1986, bought a new home in Encinitas, California, and found out their first child was on the way. Then, Kenne lost his job. "So, there I was, eight months pregnant with a huge mortgage, in total panic," Valerie says.

This tidbit of news didn't calm his new bride's fears: he wanted to start a business rather than look for another job. Kenne had grown to hate the corporate ladder in his field, and had been dreaming for years of owning a home-based business. He developed a taste for home work while at the record company, which had let him operate out of his house.

So Valerie and Kenne formed the Valerie Saint-Gaudens Jewelry Company. Kenne turned her fish pendants into a mail-order business–they found a niche by marketing jewelry to big-game fishermen.

After about a year and a half, with the business still struggling, Valerie begged Kenne to take a job with a local music company for more financial stability. "But, as the universe always does, as soon as I stopped worrying about money, business took off," Valerie says. "I had to eat my words and beg him to come home and help me with all the orders."

The best thing about forming a Home Team, Saint-Gaudens and Swink say, is freedom–a freedom they would have never known had they stayed on the corporate path. Their business success has allowed them to bring on board a jeweler and live-in maid to help with some of the day-to-day chores of home and work. Technology, too, has lent a hand, allowing their toll-free phone calls to transfer to a cellular phone during lunch trips and mini-vacations. As a result, they are able to spend plenty of time with each other and their two daughters. "I have to say that we are supremely happy doing what we are doing," Valerie says.

Couples such as Saint-Gaudens and Swink are in a prime position to design their lives the way they want them. They have established a workstyle that meets the key Home Team elements.

Requirements of this workstyle include:

- The desire and commitment to work together. We'll take a look in Chapter Three at some of the main commitments you need to make before working together in the same business.

- Similar business goals. If you decide to work together, it's vital that you're on the same page as far as business goals. If it's your lifelong dream to be a painter and your spouse's desire to be a computer consultant, chances aren't good that you will find a mix that makes you both happy. You might be better off forming the next Home Team arrangement.

- A fair amount of financial risk. If your business grows slowly or stumbles into financial troubles down the road, you might not have anything to fall back on.

- **They run separate businesses.** Mark and Susan Detwiler switched towns and homes to accommodate their businesses. Their in-state move from Warsaw, Indiana, to Fort Wayne in 1993 allowed Susan to move her information brokerage business home. Mark, who already had worked from home, continued to run his mail-order business selling collectible records.

Both agreed they didn't want to combine forces to run one business. So they set up separate home offices. Despite some initial hesitation–and some grief from associates about forming a Home Team–the Detwilers say they are happy they decided to go home. "He's more relaxed, and I'm more relaxed," Susan says.

Such an arrangement allows couples to pursue different business interests and professional goals. Some husbands and wives might long to work at home, but might be set in their ways about the type of work to pursue. Others might decide the commitment to run a business with a spouse is too strong, or that such an arrangement might not work for various reasons.

Couples in separate home businesses might spend more of the working day apart than couples who share an enterprise. This workstyle also might make it harder for couples to match schedules, whether for child care or fun together.

Requirements of this workstyle include:

• The ability to shoulder your business. Each spouse becomes like a single parent, loaded with responsibility. You will be solely responsible for making the business fly. This is especially tough in the initial years, when businesses demand a great deal of time and energy.

• A high degree of financial risk. Starting two businesses at once is a double-down bet. Solid business plans are a must. The financial risk could turn in your favor once both businesses are afloat, however, as one profitable business could help keep family finances healthy if the other enterprise struggles. Spouses who share one business don't have that option.

- The ability to mesh separate business goals and visions into a common family plan.
- The ability to be supportive when your spouse faces business challenges you might not relate to.

- **One spouse works full time in the business, the other helps part time and keeps a job outside the home.** Marjorie and Michael Desgrosseilliers were planning to have children, and several hurdles stood in the way. They wanted a better standard of living, and they realized that a business was the only vehicle to allow that to come true. They were both working full time outside the home, and they sought a lifestyle change that would accommodate children.

So, in late 1993, the Desgrosseilliers moved to Coeur d'Alene, Idaho. Marjorie, with more than ten years' experience in the research field, began AccuSearch Information Services from their new home. Michael took on a new full-time job as a home inspector but also helps his wife with her business. After some adjustments, Marjorie says they have settled into their situation well, learning a lot about each other along the way and enjoying some new-found freedoms.

The Desgrosseilliers have taken a safer route in forming a Home Team. This guarantees that a paycheck will arrive every week while Marjorie works to earn her clients' trust and bring in new business. With start-up costs and uncertainties in any business venture, a separate source of income during the early months–even years–can give entrepreneurs confidence to proceed with their dreams.

We hope, however, that couples in such an arrangement will work toward forming a full-time Home Team. Each is missing out on spending a good chunk of time most days with the other spouse, and both are living in a separate world during those job hours. A full-time job also limits these couples' freedom and minimizes or eliminates some of the other benefits we will discuss.

• **They run part-time businesses.** As with the previous Home Team option, this is a safer route financially than the first two. Husbands and wives can, in their off-work hours, build businesses to supplement their job incomes, and lay the groundwork for one or both spouses to leave their jobs in favor of the business. This plan can work for many businesses, but is especially popular today in the world of multi-level marketing, with companies such as Amway.

While part-time businesses tend to be a safe financial choice, you also have to expect slow results, as you have limited time to devote to the business. You might be able to make extra money with a part-time business, but it takes a tremendous amount of effort and energy to bring a business from startup to success in post-job hours and weekends. Many home workers start this way, however, and move into a full-time Home Team in a matter of years.

• **They telecommute.** Even if you are determined to keep working for someone else, you don't necessarily have to miss out on Home Team benefits. The number of telecommuters–corporate employees who do all or part of their work at home–has been on the rise throughout the 1990s.

What's good about telecommuting as opposed to home-based businesses? Well, the paycheck is nice. Any business owner would like to be guaranteed a certain amount in the wallet week after week. That gives telecommuters a perception of security. Couples also might be able to work together at home, which can provide benefits to the marriage and for child care.

However, there are a number of drawbacks. Most people fortunate enough to have bosses who let them telecommute must spend time at the company every week. It also might be difficult for both husband and wife to find telecommuting jobs.

Telecommuters also lack the pride of ownership that home-based business owners feel, and have less freedom to take trips and flip-flop schedules to suit their lifestyles. And, if the powers that be decide to cut the job or call a telecommuter back to the office, there isn't much recourse for the employee. Again, it's nice work if you can get it, compared to much of the job world, but the benefits are limited.

Catch the vision

At the start of this book, French author and aviator Antoine de Saint-Exupery told us that, "Life has taught us that love does not consist in gazing at each other but in looking together in the same direction." That was good advice. If he were gazing at his love, he might have flown straight into Mont Blanc. But he showed by that statement that he had a larger vision of love, one that included common hopes, goals and dreams.

The 1980s were the decade for the "me" generation, a time of greed, materialism and misplaced priorities. Flip the "m" in the 1990s, 2000s and beyond–it's time for the "we" generation. A time for love, commitment and proper focus. Today, thanks to technology, changing times and the freedoms we have in the United States, husbands and wives can turn their visions into reality. They can join together in home businesses that allow them the potential to both make a good living, and grow closer to each other and their children.

In Chapter Two, we will provide further reasons why husbands and wives should consider working at home. If you're thinking about forming a Home Team, you probably have fears and concerns that need to be addressed. You will gain a ton more confidence in the pages that follow.

Home Team Quiz 1: "How Married Are You?"

1) When was the last time you spent a day together just talking and having fun?
    a) I remember some summer day right before we got engaged ... I think we were about seventeen.
    b) Um, we had a great week-long vacation in Clearwater about two years ago ... or was it three?
    c) We try to have a date once a month, but my spouse had to work late this month ... and I had a big deadline last month ... and before that ... .
    d) Today.

2) When you spend quiet time together, what do you talk about?
    a) During those rare minutes, I ask if there are any clean clothes in the closet or check to see if the electric bill has been paid.
    b) We trade stories about those jerks at our respective offices who make our lives miserable.
    c) We try to figure out who will leave work early to see the last half of Ashley's soccer game, or whose turn it is to take the day off to watch the boys on the Casimir Pulaski school holiday.
    d) We exchange dreams about our ideal business, home and lifestyle, and make plans for how to achieve them together and enjoy more time with each other and our family.

3) How often do you kiss and say you love each other?
    a) Do what?

b) We pencil in fifteen minutes on every anniversary.

c) We call each other once a day from our separate offices and leave a message with the secretary ... both of us are too hard to reach otherwise.

d) First thing in the morning, before breakfast, after breakfast, at 10 a.m., at 11 a.m., before lunch, after lunch, at 1 p.m., at ... .

4) What do the two of you do at home ... not alone, but as a couple?

    a) Sleep.

    b) Sleep, eat dinner and watch TV.

    c) Sleep, eat dinner, watch TV and talk about work.

    d) Sleep, shower, eat breakfast, work, eat lunch, work some more, catch some afternoon rays in the backyard, prepare dinner, eat dinner, talk about our goals and dreams, read, work out, share some late-night popcorn and snuggle.

Score:

Did **a)** best match you? Have you checked lately to make sure that other person is really your spouse? You definitely need to spend more time together.

Was **b)** your choice? If your marriage were a rose bush, you might want to check for aphids–sounds like your relationship could use some nurturing.

Did you select mostly **c)**? Hey, you're trying, but something's getting in the way. Could that something be work?

Did you answer **d)**? If you're not a Home Team, you're pretty darned close. Either way, congrats!

Chapter 2

Score Another Two Touchdowns for the Home Team

Fourteen More Reasons to Love the Lifestyle

As with most people, we went into business for ourselves primarily for independence and to make more money. And we set up shop at home because we, well, couldn't afford an office in a high-rise overlooking Lake Michigan.

As time went by, however, we realized our great fortune: we had stumbled upon a special lifestyle. We backed into a way of living we never would have experienced had we continued on our career paths in the job world.

In addition to the benefits discussed in Chapter One, we have identified fourteen more perks of a successful Home Team. The benefits in this and the previous chapter are the most-cited reasons why satisfied Home Team couples say they love the arrangement and never plan to return to the traditional workforce. We will mention these reasons briefly and elaborate on them throughout the book.

1. It can deepen and strengthen your relationship, and show the world you're teammates

Unless you're playing solitaire or imitating Henry David Thoreau, most of life's games are a heck of a lot more fun when you play them with someone you love.

It's a drag to celebrate alone when you chalk up a victory in the game of life. Win a promotion or a new client at work, and, if you're lucky, someone will buy you dinner or a few drinks. Especially if you promise to stop talking about it. Although people care about you, and they are thrilled that you're happy about your success, it's difficult for them to get giddy about something that doesn't affect them.

Wouldn't it be great to have a teammate in both work and private life? Someone you love who's there to give a high-five, or raise a toast in celebration of life's victories?

And, perhaps more important, your teammate will be there at times when the wins are few. In the world outside your home, it might be difficult enough finding someone to celebrate with, but, when things go awry, even fewer folks are going to show up at your pity party.

Dan and Maureen Carlson of Prior Lake, Minnesota, say that—win or lose—they love their work-at-home arrangement. Dan runs a mail-order business selling craft supplies and educational materials. Maureen creates crafts, writes and teaches about them, and holds craft demonstrations at schools and companies. "There have been many times when one of us feels that we should quit trying to make the home business work," Dan says. "But we have overruled those feelings. We have grown close to each other in spite of, or because of, the troubles. We have to keep reminding each other of the potentials, goals and of the good times, just as any couple has to do in their marriage."

"I think it's made (our marriage) better in that we appreciate each others' strong points more," Maureen says. "I couldn't run the business without him and he couldn't run the business without me. It's like raising a child, kind of–something you're in together."

The couples we interviewed who are successful in both their working and marriage relationships struck us as different from most husbands and wives we have known. They spoke about each other with respect, sometimes almost reverence, rather than with the "ball-and-chain" attitude we've heard from far too many other couples. You also can tell by the banter between partners in a successful Home Team that they're used to working together and comfortable with each other–even when talking about personal areas of their lives.

"If you've got a healthy relationship, then a business can be a very exciting way of expressing your coupleness," says Ed Hoover, a family business consultant from the Chicago suburbs.

2. You both can live in the same world

When Jim Foy worked at a major cosmetics corporation in New York during the 1970s, it was difficult for him to relate to household challenges. After all, vital decisions–ones that involved millions of dollars and affected people's careers–were made at work every day. "It's easy to imagine that whatever is going on at home is not as important as what's going on at the office," he says.

Foy gained a different perspective on life when he began working from home with his wife. "There's just as much management involved in the home," he says, adding, "I think it's deepened our relationship." The Foys are in their third decade of marriage.

A decision to work outside the home drives a wedge between home and work life. Husbands and wives might have trouble relating to the distinct worlds that the other spouse spends much of his or her life in.

Let's say one spouse is a homemaker and the other works a conventional job. The spouse with a job thinks he's working his tail off to pay for his family's lifestyle–he's gunning hard for that promotion and better paycheck. He arrives home and is angered after finding part of the house in disarray.

"What are you doing all day–watching *Days of Our Lives?*" the husband lashes out at his wife. "You wanted to quit work and stay home with the kids. Don't you realize how hard I work? Couldn't you do just a little around here? I deserve that, don't I?"

The wife is seething. She spent the day piling in load after load of laundry, grocery shopping, taking the older kids to and from school, and chasing the babies around the house. It was one of those days during which two people wouldn't have accomplished everything.

"Don't you have any idea what goes on around here?" she snaps back. "No, of course not, because you're never around. You can't believe how much there is to do here. I'd be happy to trade places, buster–I'll bet your job is easier. I *want* to work. But I love the kids and want to care for them myself."

It's equally difficult when spouses work in different places outside the home. Each job then becomes another separate world the husband and wife cannot share.

In either scenario, typical husbands and wives are spending close to half their waking hours apart each week in activities that might produce income or self-satisfaction but do little to further their relationships. Is it any wonder we're hearing more and more people say, "My husband (or wife) and I just don't know each other anymore"?

Home Team couples might run different businesses and share different household responsibilities. And couples vary regarding how distinct their home and work lives are. But, day after day, they're living in the same world.

"Working together is just an amazing way to integrate your lives," Jim Foy says.

3. You can gain a better grasp on your priorities in life

When we worked outside the home, it was hard to focus on what was important. Every day, it seemed, some other ridiculous crisis took top priority: When is our department going to be reorganized? Did you hear the Chicago office's budget is twice as large as ours? What's up with all these salary-freeze rumors? And who the heck keeps stealing the scissors from everyone's desk?

Working at home together gives you the opportunity to view life from a new perspective. We sometimes get a kick out of reminiscing about all the things that used to get us worked up at our jobs. At the time, they seemed so vital to our futures. In retrospect, they were just plain silly.

Besides the perception that every decision carried the importance of the next step in a minefield, there are two other destructive forces in the workplace that we don't miss: office politics and gossip.

Both of us have sworn that neither has plans to dethrone or undermine the other. And the only gossiping we can do in the home workplace is about the dogs. ("Did you hear about Taffy? She dirtied the carpet again while you were gone.") Office politics and water-cooler gossip are energy- and attitude-draining poison, and we're glad to have them out of our lives. With those aside, it's easier to concentrate on work or other tasks before it's time to enjoy family fun.

Despite the challenges of self-employment, we've become more relaxed since we left the workforce. That's mainly because our top three priorities suddenly became crystal clear: God, family and work.

When you work together, you are reminded of what's important daily.

What are your priorities? Are you spending enough time in those areas?

4. Your co-worker is prequalified

Ever since you started dating, there have been reasons why you have been crazy about one person and not another. After you get appearance and personality requirements–whatever they might be–out of the way, why you like someone boils down to a handful of qualities you can clearly identify and a slew more you might never be able to explain but consider vital. As time passes and the relationship grows, those qualities will help you decide whether your significant other is THE one.

Unfortunately, you don't have the pleasure of the same screening process in the traditional work world. You get to share time and space with whoever is occupying the adjacent desk, no matter how poorly the two of you might get along. Even if you hired the person and were initially overwhelmed with positive impressions, odds are that–over the long haul–there's someone else in the world you would relate to better and rather be with. With a co-worker, you're stuck–even if he imitates *Saturday Night Live* characters or pops gum all day. You might be together dozens of hours a week for years to come. Yeah, that's the ticket!

We'll assume the reason you tied the knot with your spouse is you were madly in love. If you married for money or as part of some other sinister plot, chances are good you're not reading this book. You're probably watching *Montel* and waiting, pen in hand, for information about how to be a future guest.

In addition to all the magical qualities that combine to equal love, there are probably some good, logical reasons you chose him or her as a spouse. Is your spouse someone you respect? Trust? Does he or she have great integrity? Smarts? Loyalty? Do you have fun together?

"We have a pretty good time together–we appreciate each other's sense of humor," says James Patterson about working with his wife, Toby Myles. They run a graphic design and marketing communications business from their Olney, Maryland, home. "I'd just as soon work with her as much as anyone."

What traits would you look for in a business partner or co-worker? Perhaps your search is done.

5. You will see qualities in your spouse that will amaze you

Patterson and Myles say working together magnified each other's talents: "You see strengths and weaknesses in a different atmosphere," Patterson says. "You see things that many husbands and wives might not appreciate–like I saw Toby's skill with people and her design skills. You can work different jobs and talk about those things over dinner, but we get to see it in a different environment."

If people at your spouse's workplace run into you at the Christmas party and tell you how efficient your wife is at work, it's never going to mean as much as regularly seeing the results yourself. It's like the difference between hearing about a Picasso sculpture and seeing it firsthand–the latter might leave you with a great appreciation for that work, while the former leaves you asking, "The fork is *where*?"

Colette and Ed Hoover say working together has given them a greater appreciation for each other. They ran their consulting business from home for three years before moving to an office in Oakbrook Terrace, Illinois. When they explain that they work together, the response they often hear is, "Don't you lose your individuality that way?"

"We found in our work that, when we spend a lot of time together, the opposite happened," Ed says. "We have become more aware of our individuality because we work together. We see our strengths and weaknesses. You have to learn to respect each other in a whole new way." If husbands and wives don't grow close enough, he adds, they can't say, "I really respect what you do."

When you are working together successfully, you will see new, wonderful qualities in your spouse as well as daily reinforcements for those you have grown to love.

6. You can't be fired

One of the best parts of being in business for yourselves is the feeling of control. When you work for someone else–whether you're the CEO or the janitor–your future is out of your hands, even if you're the best at what you do. A corporate reorganization, staff cutbacks, office politics or poorly timed mistake are just some of the excuses that can catapult you to the unemployment line.

There is no such thing as a secure job.

All through our childhoods, teachers told us we should study hard to get good grades. That would get us into good universities, where, if we studied hard some more, we would receive the diplomas that would land us fantastic jobs that would make us giddy with happiness and financial security for the rest of our lives.

The two of us followed that plan religiously. So much so that it made us both sick because of stress at points in our lives. But instead of reaping great rewards as we entered the job world, we found ourselves scratching our heads for years, trying to figure out what was wrong with the plan.

Neither of us was making enough money, and both lost jobs for reasons that had nothing to do with performance.

Not one educator–ever–stressed we should consider working for ourselves.

Why? We guess it's like the story of a mom and her daughter preparing a holiday meal. The daughter puts the ham in a pan, and her mom says, "Wait, you have to cut the end off first." The daughter asks her mom why, and she responds, "That's the way my mom taught me." So they call Grandma, and she has the same response. Finally, Grandma visits her mother to solve this great mystery. "Why did you used to cut the end off the ham before you put it in the pan?" she asks. The wise old lady shakes her head and laughs: "Because my pan wasn't big enough."

Why didn't any of our schoolday mentors tell us to consider self-employment? Probably because they worked for someone else, and that's all they knew. No wonder it's so hard for most people to think beyond the job mentality–that's the way most of us have been programmed throughout our lives.

Jim and Michelle Foy of Winnetka, Illinois, work as management consultants to small businesses and not-for-profits, and construct computer databases. They started their business from home in 1980 and both have been full time since 1985. Five years later, Jim was struck with a revelation. Michelle recalls the moment: "He looked at me and said, 'It just dawned on me–nobody can fire me.'"

"That's a considerable advantage in this particular economy," Jim adds. "We can lose a client, but we're not going to lose them all."

Despite the financial unknowns that self-employment brings, there's great peace in knowing that, while your spouse might beg you to clean off your desk, no one can make you clean it out.

7. Your kids will appreciate it

A little now and a lot more when they are adults.

While it might be frustrating for kids to understand why Mommy or Daddy can't be bothered at all times when they are in the home, these children will grow up knowing both of their parents were present and more involved in their upbringing than most parents are.

As kids grow older, they also will appreciate knowing more about what their parents do for a living. When we were kids, our moms and dads were always curious about how our friends' parents made a living–they wanted a better idea of who we were hanging out with. We'd always ask our friends and get answers such as, "Dad does something with the government" or "Mom does something at some office." These responses made for lame reports back home.

On the other hand, when parents work at home, their kids will acquire a firm grasp of what Mom and Dad do every day. Children can see their parents working together for their collective futures, and some parents might even choose to involve their kids in the businesses.

Combine a business in the home with loving parents working and having fun together, and you have a vehicle for teaching kids values and sharing experiences that can last a lifetime.

8. You can design your own workdays

None of our bosses ever asked what our ideal schedules would be. They never inquired when we would be most alert and likely to perform our best, or were concerned about our convenience.

Most jobs dictate where you need to be and when you need to be there, regardless of your biorhythms or family's schedule. Although we're hearing more about "flex-time"–which gives employees options of times to report to work–it isn't prevalent and doesn't provide the consistent flexibility of home-based self-employment.

Are you a morning person? Some people, as they used to say in those U.S. Army commercials, can do more before 9 a.m. than most people do all day. Perhaps you're a night owl and can't get cranking until long after dinner. Either way, you're out of luck if you're a typical 8-to-5er.

If it were up to you, when would you work? (No, "never" isn't an option.) Most work-at-home professions offer the flexibility to do some or all of the work when you choose.

Imagine not having to worry about taking time off work for doctor or dentist appointments. Perhaps your engine runs out in the afternoon and could be jump-started with a quick nap that would make you super effective for the rest of the workday. When can time be set aside each day for either home or personal tasks? When you work for yourself at home, it's your call. When you work for someone else, it's theirs.

9. *You might become wealthy*

Money should never be the main reason you decide to do anything in life. If it is, you're going to end up feeling empty in the long run–regardless of whether you get it. What money can do is pay bills, build security for yourself and the ones you love, and allow you and your family to have some fun in this wacky world.

Can you become wealthy working a job? Few people do so. Most struggle financially their whole lives, and a small percentage get comfortable, but few get rich. A millionaire colleague once told us, if you don't believe that, find people vacationing at an exclusive tropical paradise or sailing on their yachts, and ask them who they work for. He guarantees their answers will be identical: "I work for no man, my friend. I work for myself."

Those who would still argue that a job is the right road in life have to concede this statement: No one with a job is free. If you're a surgeon making a six-figure income or a guy slinging burgers for five bucks an hour, your schedule is not under your control. You live for weekends and vacation time, and pray you're alive and healthy come retirement age to reap the benefits of a life's work.

Only those who work for themselves can become wealthy *and* free.

Your long-term income when you work at home is based largely on your decisions of what businesses to run, how you conduct your businesses, and how hard you persevere, rather than how much a boss decides you're worth. Nothing is guaranteed in life. But your financial future lies more in your hands, which can be terrifying or exciting, whichever way you look at it.

Also, remember that our tax laws are structured to benefit businesses. When you run a business from home, bills you have been throwing money at for years–including utilities, cars and travel–become partially tax deductible, as long as they play legitimate roles in your businesses. Learn as much as you can about our tax laws and find a tax adviser who knows the ins and outs of home-based businesses.

Add potential tax benefits to the money you will save in areas such as commuting, business clothes and lunches out every day, and your family's bottom line might increase. Remember, as the saying goes, "It's not what you make, it's what you keep."

If you are not convinced you could get wealthy running a home-based business, how would you feel if you only equaled your current job salaries? Or, let's take a pessimistic view and ask this question: Would you take a pay cut to leave your job and work at home so you could pursue a business dream, or spend more time with your spouse and kids?

We didn't have to, but we gladly would have. Wouldn't it be worth it?

Now *that's* wealth.

10. Your home turns into an even better investment

You will be spending much more of your life at home, so it had better be a place you enjoy. And, in the long term, you will need somewhere to work other than the kitchen table, or at a desk next to boxes of Christmas decorations in the basement. You wouldn't put up with those conditions very long at a job, so why subject yourself to them at home?

When you work at home, a smart investment in your house becomes an investment in yourself and your business. If the end result makes you more effective, productive and profitable, the investment makes sense from a business standpoint. In the early stages of business, a great deal of money shouldn't be spent on remodeling and furniture–a mistake many small-business owners make. Funds are better used in making sure the business becomes profitable and maintains a good cash flow.

The key is to start small and build ambiance. Wallpaper or a fresh coat of paint in the home office can do wonders on a limited budget. Hang paintings of beautiful, faraway places as well as pictures of the ones you love. And don't forget an underestimated but vital component to the home office: a window. Birds, trees–even the screaming kids next door–are often helpful reminders that life goes on outside the home office.

As your incomes grow, you might think bigger. Perhaps you would like an addition to the home to house the entire business operation in one spot. Renovations to the house that have no direct impact on your businesses also might be more readily welcome when both husband and wife work at home. When one spouse wants new curtains and a remodeled kitchen, the other is more likely to question the expense if he or she is never around to enjoy those.

Do you want a small garden pool with a waterfall and giant Japanese Koi goldfish? That might sound frivolous if you're not home much, but it could be a soothing and worthwhile addition if you work at home.

It's exciting to see that the real estate crowd has come around and is touting home offices as a key selling point. If your businesses are stable and your home isn't suited to your workstyles, check out other existing homes or have one built to meet your needs and wants. Whatever your budget dictates, you can make parts of your home more enjoyable now and add improvements or move later.

Home is as much a wonderful retreat as a work environment for Ronald Lee Fleming and Renata von Tscharner, who have run a public interest planning organization, Townscape Institute, from their Cambridge, Massachusetts, residence since 1979. They have filled their house, near Harvard Square, with antiques and paintings they love, and have added a hot tub and garden for additional relaxation and pleasure.

Still, a house need not be ideal to make working at home together successful and pleasurable. One couple we interviewed runs writing and computer consulting businesses from their four-hundred-fifty-square-foot home in California. They say they are having the time of their lives. That's one close couple.

11. You can help each other grow personally and professionally

Marjorie Desgrosseilliers knew better than to talk back to bosses at her former jobs. Even if she disagreed vehemently with her superiors' "suggestions," experience taught her the best place to spout unsolicited opinions was under her breath rather than through her mouth.

But when she began working at home with her husband and business partner, Michael, her views flowed more freely. If your business partner's an equal and also happens to be your spouse, he can take it, right?

"Who do you think you are telling *me* what to do?" Marjorie recalls as her reaction to Michael's suggestions as they started their information brokerage business from their Coeur d'Alene, Idaho, home in 1993. "My biggest problem with working together is not to let ego get in the way," Marjorie says. "When you're working as husband and wife, you have to keep emotions out of the way. It's still something I'm working on."

She can't say enough about her husband's patience during those times. If she snapped at him to go away, he'd usually do so without argument. He gave her time to grow into the new working environment as each of them discovered magnified personality traits, including Marjorie's need for independence.

When you work together, there's plenty of need for understanding and growth. It's fun to watch your spouse face challenges and become a better person, and to see him or her improve professionally. It's also satisfying to know that you can play a role in helping your spouse grow.

"It has helped us develop respect and patience with each other," Marjorie says. "We didn't have to deal with that before–we showed emotions we didn't even know existed. Because every decision you make is important."

For Home Teams, decisions are important. And because that's true ...

12. You will have more to talk about

Guaranteed. Boy, will you have plenty to talk about.

If couples ever find themselves chatting about nothing more than reportage–that is, the weather, what happened today, Uncle Fred's prostate troubles, last night's episode of *Melrose Place*–perhaps it's a sign they don't have enough in common.

The sign glows neon when couples don't talk much at all.

Spend more time with your spouse and add businesses to the homestead, and you will rarely scramble for topics of conversation.

If your businesses and relationship are growing, you can bet one major reason is because you're talking–communicating beyond superficial levels. Talking about dreams your businesses will bring to life. Talking about your goals, and assessing strategies to meet those. Talking about clients. Talking about who's going to watch the kids and who's going to mow the lawn. Talking about your love for each other.

Talking about the good times and the challenges.

13. You can have more fun

Forming a Home Team provides incredible opportunities for spontaneity. On a sunny day, you both can sneak away to enjoy a walk in the park or a swim. If you don't want to leave work entirely, you might be able to transfer your calls to your cellular phone and head out to enjoy the day with your significant other or the kids. We'll talk about many other getaway ideas in a later chapter, "Getting Away From It All When It's All at Home."

14. You have more chances for romance and sex

Some couples also say that working together at home has done wonders for their love life, both in sheer attraction and time available for lovin'. The afternoon escape to the bedroom or office surprise can spice up a drab workday in a big way. We'll discuss this in detail in the chapter, "Fooling Around at the Office."

Now that we have examined more of the potential benefits of forming a Home Team, let's take an in-depth look at the commitments you must make before deciding to work together, as well as how to get started properly should you choose to proceed.

Home Team Quiz 2: "Why Start a Home Team?"

1) Why are you thinking about changing your lifestyle?
   a) Because my boss hates me and is probably ready to fire me any day now–I need something to fall back on.
   b) Because my parents have always told me I should run my own business.
   c) Because my spouse hates the hours and demands of my work.
   d) Because I want to control my own career and enjoy life with my spouse and kids.

2) Why did you marry your spouse?
   a) She isn't at all like my mother/He isn't at all like my father.
   b) Everyone likes her/him.
   c) She's pretty and she's a good caretaker and mom/He's handsome and he's a good provider and dad.
   d) She/he is my soulmate and we want to spend the rest of our lives together.

3) Why have you stayed married?
   a) Because I couldn't stand the thought of being single again.
   b) Because everyone else in my family has been divorced, and I don't want to be like them.
   c) Because we get along OK, we're used to each other and we have kids together.

Score Another Two

d) Because we love each other–even when we argue or get angry–and we committed to each other "until death do us part."

4) What would be your ideal career?
   a) To win twenty million dollars and never have to do anything again in my life.
   b) To become a hotshot with a fat paycheck, fancy car and giant house.
   c) To call my own shots and never have to work for a jerk again.
   d) To call my own shots, do something I love and enjoy, make a decent living doing it and share that success with my spouse, family and friends.

Score:

Did you choose mostly **a)**? Sounds as if you're seeking escape from some negatives in your life–is a Home Team really what you want to escape to, though?

Was **b)** the best match? Hey, these are *your* lives we're talking about here. Stop worrying about what other people think–and then decide if the Home Team lifestyle can give you what you want.

Did you answer **c)**? You're halfway there, but you need to dig deeper if you're going to have the motivation to become a Home Team.

Was your choice **d)**? Bingo! You've got the right reasons for starting a Home Team.

Chapter 3
Home Team Fundamentals

As with skydiving, the ballet and haggis, working at home is not for everyone. Neither is working as a Home Team. So before you decide to work together, you need to take an honest look at your relationship to see if the arrangement is right for you.

Colette and Ed Hoover, who provide consulting services to family businesses and also started out working at home, say couples thinking about launching a shared business need to look at past experiences with other joint projects. "Have you redecorated or built a house together?" Colette asks. "How did it go?"

It's not important to have the "perfect marriage" to be a Home Team. If you know what the perfect marriage is, by the way, drop us a line, because we haven't a clue. Many types of marriage relationships are successful. For Home Team purposes, your potential hinges more on compatibility: Have you been able to join forces successfully in past endeavors–whether planning a party or deciding what house to buy?

Home Team Fundamentals

Do you work well together in "non-fun" things? Going to the beach or out to dinner together is easy. But have you worked well together in solving a discipline problem with your kids, building a patio or shopping for a birthday present for a difficult-to-please parent? It doesn't mean that you never disagreed during the project–just that you were able to work through the differences and achieve results you were both satisfied with, in a manner you were both satisfied with.

You don't have to agree all the time or think identically. Far from it. As Ed and Colette built their business, they learned more about what made them different from each other, more about the talents and skills that were uniquely his or hers. Working together need not erase your personalities and turn the two of you into some freakish, two-headed creature, in which no one can tell where you end and your spouse begins.

Successful Home Teams are made up of two distinct but complementary people, partners who can contribute different perspectives, ideas and skills to a joint venture and create something greater than they could on their own. Handled correctly, the arrangement can bring out the best in both of you.

On the other hand, in the wrong circumstances, it also can bring out the worst in two people. That's why a Home Team is not usually the answer for a couple looking to rescue a faltering relationship. Ed Hoover says he has seen instances where a couple will think just that–"We're having trouble, so maybe working together will help us." Wrong. "If you've got marriage problems, a business is going to make it worse," he adds. People with severe marriage woes need professional counseling, not a home business.

Of course, there are rare exceptions, such as one couple we spoke with who began working together as a last resort for saving their marriage. In their case, creating a Home

Team solved the biggest problem plaguing their relationship: a lack of common pursuits. Both had been working so intensely at their jobs, they didn't have the time or energy to share life with each other. For them, joining forces in business improved their marriage.

Say your vows

Ready to form a Home Team? Not quite yet. It's one of the biggest commitments you will make in your life. With that in mind, a set of vows is in order. While there's no magic formula for success, we have found that adherence to these statements will give you a good start and allow you to handle just about anything that fate tosses your way. Established Home Teams, this is your chance for a second Home Team marriage with your spouse. Who needs Vegas?

In either an actual or mental activity, put on your best sweat suits (home work attire) and approach the door to your present or future home office. Remove the dust jacket from this book and tape our picture to the doorway–we'll preside over the ceremony. (Our likenesses are permitted to perform legal Home Team partnership ceremonies in all respectable parts of the world. If prohibited where you live, move immediately.)

Join hands and face the door. If you need elaboration on any of the vows, skip immediately to the explanations that follow the ceremony. One spouse, repeat after us ...

"I, (STATE YOUR NAME), take you, (SPOUSE'S NAME HERE), to be my Home Team partner. In the presence of God and the photo of these authors, I state with full sincerity:

- "I am fully committed to our relationship, and I love you with all my heart;
- "I want to work at home with you;

- "I respect you now and will always strive to treat you with respect;
- "I will commit to personal and professional growth, and will work hard to better ensure our special relationship and businesses are successful;
- "I will be patient and forgiving, and will communicate openly, honestly and lovingly with you about business and personal matters."

Now, your partner's turn.

Are you both still there, or has one of you raced down the hallway and scurried back to the job world? If you're both present, *We now pronounce you a Home Team.* Kiss your spouse and take turns carrying each other across the office threshold. Celebrate with a beverage of your choice and a hot bath, which also will alleviate back pain from the previous instruction. Have someone take a photo of the two of you in your office sometime in the next few days, and please remember to mail us a copy at the address listed in the back of the book.

Hope you had fun with the Home Team ceremony. But remember: You must be able to make these statements with full sincerity. These will lay the foundation for a successful working relationship. No matter how solid your marriage is, being a successful Home Team is NOT EASY. Anyone who would state the above vows only halfheartedly would be better off sticking to more conventional ways of making a living. Business ownership is challenging enough–when you enter this workstyle as well, all the idiosyncrasies each of you has, all the different personality traits, become quickly apparent, and you must deal with them properly.

This, however, is part of the beauty of Home Teams. You can share more of life's experiences, and help your relationship develop to a higher level–if you accept both personal growth and flexibility as part of a mature and successful marriage.

Let's examine each of the vows in more detail:

I am fully committed to our relationship, and I love you with all of my heart. Obvious, right? Maybe, but this one is the most important of all. We all will slip up in the other vows at one time or another. But there's no room for error on this one. Choose to duck out on your spouse or decide it's time in your life for a little hanky-panky with someone else, and you'll experience the exhilaration of ruining both your family AND your career. If you are not one hundred percent committed to each other, it is a bad idea to work at home together. There simply is too much on the line.

Should unmarried couples form a Home Team? Every situation is different, but the answer usually is no. Unless there are rare, extenuating circumstances that are delaying or preventing you from marrying, this workstyle usually is best reserved for those who have made a lifelong commitment. Again, both your personal and professional lives are in the balance. If unmarried spouses decide they want to form a Home Team, they certainly would be better off running separate businesses than becoming full partners. That would make matters easier should they decide to go their separate ways.

I want to work at home with you. Are you looking forward to being a Home Team, or is one of you only grudgingly giving it a try because your spouse wants to do it? This arrangement requires an enthusiastic commitment from both partners. It takes a firm belief that this will be good for both of you as individuals and as a married couple. Everyone has fears of the unknown–that's to be expected. But if you have doubts about whether you want to work with your spouse, it would be better to take some time and think about the idea.

I respect you now and will always strive to treat you with respect. Even if you've spent most of your working lives in different spheres, can you look at your spouse and honestly say you admire his or her skills, accomplishments and way of doing things? If you think highly of each other as people, chances are you've got a strong foundation for the Home Team lifestyle, no matter how different your personalities, education or experiences may be. Those with a propensity to inflict physical or mental abuse on their spouses under no circumstances should work together.

I will commit to personal and professional growth, and will work hard to better ensure our special relationship and businesses are successful. Growing both a successful business and Home Team partnership takes time. Will you invest the time, money and energy needed for a serious effort at victory? Finding your particular styles of working together might take awhile–you shouldn't think about calling it quits after three weeks just because both of you had a bad day and took it out on each other.

Home Team couples must make a conscious effort to make their businesses and relationships better every day, rather than just "letting things happen." Nothing is guaranteed in life, but there's a strong correlation between good old sweat equity and success in both a business and a marriage.

Commit to reading informative books and publications, taking classes and seminars–anything that will teach you how to become a better business owner and marriage partner. When people talk of investments, most of the focus is on stocks, bonds, mutual funds and the like. They're important, but an investment in yourself is one of the greatest you can make. Consider contributing about five percent of your income toward personal and professional growth.

I will be patient and forgiving, and will communicate openly, honestly and lovingly with you about business and

personal matters. At times, you are going to mess up, and mess up good. How are you going to react when your spouse errs? Name-calling, finger-pointing, tantrums, fits and pouting won't help you in the home office any more than they will in the kitchen, living room or bedroom. You wouldn't act this way in the workplace, so don't do it at home. Go a step further–treat each other even better than you would treat co-workers. After all, your Home Teammate is the one person you will be sleeping with after work, and you want to keep it that way.

Getting started

If you have taken the leap and formed a Home Team or have renewed your Home Team vows, congratulations! Now, it's time to move on to steps you can take that will help you both at the start and over the long haul.

Atop the list of stress-creating situations in life, changing jobs ranks right up there with the death of a loved one, illness and changing residences. And that's just for the process of leaving one established workplace to join another, where you have a good chance of knowing what your new title, duties and salary will be. What about the person–or couple–who leaves a familiar, predictable job for the strange, new, no-boundaries, impossible-to-predict world of the work-at-home entrepreneur? Now *that's* stress.

Don't panic, though. There are ways to prepare for the change that can help you avoid some of the bumpiest spots. If you have the time before starting a home business, for example, it's smart to save up at least a few months' salary to tide you over while your business is taking its baby steps. You will also do yourself a favor by learning as much as you can about the how-tos of running a home business. (Check "Recommended Reading" at the end of this book for some great resources in such areas as how to set up a home office, buy the right equipment, market your new venture, and find health insurance, support services and business networking opportunities.) Doing your homework and putting the advice into action is the best way to up your chances of business success.

But beyond those kinds of nuts and bolts, you will need to prepare for other adjustments, such as: learning how to get yourself into–and out of–the office at a reasonable hour every day; teaching yourself to be tough with people who interrupt you because they can't understand you're really working while you're at home; coming to terms with the fact that you are now everything in your business–purchaser, billing manager, marketing director, even janitor. Basically, you have to get ready to make the mental leap from employee to entrepreneur. These life issues that we'll focus on are every bit as important as the business-end tidbits you must learn from other work-at-home books.

In the ideal Home Team world, every couple would have plenty of time to plan and launch their home business; ample cash in the bank; a profitable troop of clients lined up; a modern, ergonomic and spacious home office designed just for them; and a clear idea of what they will be doing and where they are going.

In the real world, it's rarely that easy.

Thanks to today's ever-evolving and unsettled marketplace, many home entrepreneurs get their start through pink slips rather than preference. After one, two, even three or more encounters with layoffs, downsizing, restructuring, right-sizing, getting the shaft–whatever you want to call it–some folks decide they have had enough. They conclude the job world isn't as secure as people make it out to be and they opt for self-employment as a chance to better control their futures.

Dan Carlson, for example, decided to follow his wife's lead and started working at their Prior Lake, Minnesota, home after he was laid off in 1989. Maureen had created crafts and sold her work at shows for fifteen years at that point–she stayed home from her teaching job after their children were born. After losing his full-time job, Dan had a chance for another position, but instead chose to join Maureen and create a new part of the business: while she designed crafts and taught craft techniques, he launched an offshoot focusing on mail-order marketing of craft supplies. "When he got laid off, it was an incentive to make this work," Maureen says.

Aron Shtull-Trauring, who works with his wife, Simcha, from their home in Kokhav Yair, Israel, encountered an eye-opening, double-whammy in the corporate world. He had spent years in software development, international marketing and sales, but discovered the hard way that his skills did not guarantee job security.

"After being laid off once, and when Simcha was looking for a new career, I encouraged her to start a multimedia business," he recalls. She did, which provided him with a new career opportunity. "When I got laid off a second time I decided–with her encouragement–to join the business full time."

Others have been lucky enough to dodge the corporate bullet so far, but aren't sure how long their luck will hold out. Or maybe they've just always wanted to run their own businesses, and the time seems right.

Michelle and Jim Foy were looking for a better, more family-friendly lifestyle when they made preparations to start their home business. He was working for a cosmetics company in New York City at the time, but both of them wanted out.

"We decided raising our kids in New York was not what we wanted to do," Jim recalls. A transfer to Chicago also raised the specter of "corporate suicide"–New York City was *the* place for employees in his line of work to be, and the

Foys found themselves fending off repeated offers to return there. Inspired by friends who were starting their own businesses, the Foys decided to start working as management consultants–she jumped in right away full time and he did what he could part time. Finally, after more than five years, a corporate plan to move all of Jim's department back to New York prompted his decision to go for severance and take a chance on full-time self-employment with Michelle.

"All of a sudden, the horizon got very close," Jim recalls. "I'd always been at a point where I could see my career (end)–retirement, a condo in Florida in the future. (My employer) was a very stable, big company. Now, I was responsible for all of it. For me, that was an adjustment."

Vicki and Steve Palmquist also eased into their Home Team arrangement. In their case, she had been running a writing and desktop publishing venture from home when business grew too busy. Vicki needed help, but the zoning in their neighborhood prevented her from hiring an employee. Rented office space elsewhere also was out of the question–she enjoyed her home office too much to leave. So the natural step was for Steve to quit work at a fruit-breeding research center and join her in the business. It was a decision neither regrets.

However it happens–planned or by chance–you must make sure you're on the same wavelength in your business and personal lives.

The grand plans

The quiet evenings you set aside to form your business and life plans are among the most important in your Home Team relationship. Please, do not make the mistake of passing these by.

People have a tendency to think, "I know what I want." But, too often, they don't take the time to think their desires through past the superficial level. Then, years later, they find themselves unsatisfied, scratching their heads about what went wrong. Rather than following a game plan for their businesses and relationships, those who don't develop a vision in these areas instead end up going through life as directionless as a drunk fresh off a Tilt-a-Whirl. If you are an existing Home Team and have never developed plans, now is the perfect time to do so.

Your plans don't have to look like annual reports, but they have to be written. This will allow you to refer to them later, so you can make changes and additions as your businesses grow and your dreams evolve. Perhaps the furthest you can see now is matching your previous job income within the first year and achieving a ten-percent hike the next year. That's a great start. But, a few years down the road, who knows? Your dreams might expand to include a new house or exotic travel. No matter how good your memory is, commit your plans to paper. You will be glad you did.

Dedicate at least one evening–preferably more–to each of the following four exercises. You may ask each other questions as you go, but try to do the first three exercises individually so you will have thought through the important points before discussing them.

1. Answer one simple but vital question: "Why am I doing this?" What are all the things you want out of home-based self-employment? Answers such as "money" are not enough. Why do you want more money? What will that enable you to do? Every time you write down a response, continue to ask yourself "why" until you get to the true answer. You need to develop a crystal-clear vision of why you are starting a home business, and what you want it to do for your family life, as well. Don't take this question lightly–it is vital. If you can't answer this question from the heart now, the challenges you will face down the road might conquer your spirit and run you out of business.

2. Develop your business plan. Every serious business needs a plan. Whether the plan is two pages or two hundred, it needs to spell out important details, such as your company's mission statement, financial projections, marketing plans, and goals along with dates you plan to reach them. These will help you keep your business on track. Do your homework, write the plan, then execute it. Set your goals high, but make them reachable to avoid discouragement.

Plenty of small-business books will walk you through the particulars of a business plan if you need additional help writing one. For our purposes, we will focus primarily on how the business plan plays into your relationship.

If you run separate businesses, spell out the areas in which there will be crossover. If you are building the same business, how will the responsibilities be divvied up?

And, a big one: "Who makes the decisions, big and small?" Couples handle this issue in a variety of ways, and it's a sure bet this is an instance in which people will dig in their heels and insist their way is right. In some cases, one spouse works for the other, so it is clear where the buck stops. But many Home Team couples today enter business as equal partners. In that case, what will you do if there is a clear split of opinion about a business purchase? Do nothing? Best-out-of-three, "paper, rock, scissors"? Arm wrestle? Flip a coin?

You need to develop a clear system now, rather than when the first major crisis strikes. We will discuss this topic in greater detail in the next chapter about your relationship–you might want to flip ahead now for ideas on how other couples deal with this issue.

3. Develop your life plan. A home business will affect most aspects of your life. Thinking beforehand about what you want and what you are willing to sacrifice or change in the quest to get it will help keep everything in perspective.

Sacrifice and flexibility are major keys to a successful Home Team relationship, especially in the early months–perhaps even years–that tend to be especially stressful and tumultuous.

A life plan should answer questions such as:

• How will you handle responsibilities if a family crisis arises–if one of you has to stop working temporarily, will you be willing and able to keep running the business as well as handle other domestic matters?

• What about the future? Do you always want to run the same business, or do you want to branch out into other ventures? Is your dream to always work at home, or do you want to start there and build a megacorporation with thousands of employees? Would it bother you to have employees in your home business at some point?

• What is your tolerance for financial risk? How far in debt will you go to make your business work? Will you take on a home equity loan, or a home equity line of credit? Borrow money from your friends, relatives or investors? Go into credit card debt? How much of your personal and retirement savings are you willing to invest in your business? Financial arguments are among the most common a couple will have in their lives. With the unknowns of business life, it is important to agree how far you will go in your quest to make your businesses work.

• How important are vacations, and when should you take them? Will you cut back on or eliminate vacations in the short term to get your businesses rolling?

• Will you build a business your kids can inherit if they want to? What about the kids now–do you want them involved in the business in any way?

• Would you move to a smaller home temporarily to decrease overhead? Give up your vacation home? Get rid of a second car? Dine out less frequently?

These are relationship- and lifestyle-oriented questions that don't always come up in business plans, but they are vital for Home Teams to answer.

A life plan can be broken down into these areas:
- Your working relationship. What if you have separate businesses and one fails while the other succeeds? Would one of you consider joining the other's thriving business? You should each have a clear idea of what your boundaries and expectations will be, and make sure your partner understands them as well.
- Priorities. How do kids, pets, household duties and responsibilities to other family members fit into your plans? Is one of you willing to play a reduced role in the business to raise children, or would you rather find an alternative that gives you both equal work responsibilities? What's more important–a spotless kitchen and three home-cooked meals a day, or a full-time commitment to the business, no matter how grungy the house might get at times? Do you have a plan for how you both would keep the business going if an aging parent moves in and requires a great deal of help?

Couples who fail to consider family questions might learn the hard way that they have different ideas about what's important when it comes to blending work and homelife. It's best to know from the beginning that you are willing to put up with an unmade bed and an occasional sinkful of dirty dishes, but your partner will go crazy if everything isn't neat and in its place. That way, you can try to hammer out a solution that works for both of you before either gets too stressed.
- Your non-working relationship. How will your business affect the rest of your life together? Do both of you expect to start work and finish at the same time every day, or are you more interested in working according to your individual time clocks? Is it important that there's a guaranteed time when you won't talk shop at home, no matter how pressing

a business problem might be? Both of you need to prepare for how work will impact the rest of your life, because it will. And, if you're not careful, it can take over the rest of your life, for better or for worse.

• Your work's effect on others. Are you prepared to set strict rules about when family and friends can visit, even though you're at home every day and always enjoy company? How important is it to get together regularly with old friends from work now that you no longer work with them? Setting up shop at home can change relationships with people who are used to seeing you in an outside office and don't quite understand the "work-at-home thing." The two of you need to reach decisions on how to accommodate other people in your lives while leaving enough time for work, each other, your kids and yourself.

4. Compare your plans. Go through each of the plans and discuss your thoughts in detail. Bet you will be in for some surprises. You will find many common dreams and goals, but you also will see areas in which you fall on different ends of the spectrum. You're not required to agree on every point, but you should reach a level of understanding and figure out if compromise is possible, or brainstorm to see if there is another alternative that is better for you both. If there are too many issues in which you don't see eye to eye, take more time to talk about matters before heading full steam into your businesses.

Remember, though, that no matter how well you plan, things change. People develop different interests and priorities as time goes by, unexpected developments can radically alter your family life, and your business itself can transform into something wildly different from what you planned. You can't prepare for everything, but examining a lot of the what-ifs beforehand will help when situations arise. Be open with each other about your needs and wants, not just now but every day for the rest of your lives. Look at your life plan as an ever-evolving set of goals and dreams, rather than a rigid outline carved in granite.

An al dente lifestyle: firm but flexible

Pasta is a good menu choice when you go out to eat: Most places know how to prepare it properly, and, with the right sauces or seasonings, it can make a tasty and healthful meal. It's also a good model for your work-at-home lifestyle.

Why? Because your approach toward work and the rest of your life should be firm but flexible, like an al dente pasta. A well-cooked noodle won't refuse to bend when you bite into it, as a grain of rice does, but it won't be mushy, either. It gives when it has to, wrapping nicely around a fork when you prepare to take a taste, but doesn't lose its shape entirely. Cooked or uncooked, every kind of pasta retains its basic character–you can always tell a rotini from a spaghettini, a fusilli from a ziti. In the same way, the well-prepared Home Team can bend and adapt when situations demand, but it also knows when to stand firm and steady.

When you start working together at home, you need to establish boundaries to figure out where you're willing to adjust and where you're not. That's because the work-at-home world, unlike offices you've worked at, has no built-in rules. The nice part is, you get to set your own rules. The tough part is, you get to set your own rules.

Suddenly, we're weirdos

One of the peculiar situations you need to prepare for upon becoming a Home Team is the unsolicited baffled, astounded and uncomprehending remarks you'll get from relatives, friends and assorted bystanders. As common as the home office is becoming, most people out there still do their weekly forty-plus in a traditional workplace, and home-based self-employment can be a hard concept for them to grasp.

Anyone who works at home will attract her share of doubtful glances and commentary from concerned family members and buddies. They're just *sure* your chipper assertions that "things are going great" are really a brave front from someone who's desperately unemployed but can't find a "real" job. Even if they secretly envy your work-at-home lifestyle, people *will* feel they are required to pity you, at least until your business has been up and running for a few years and is clearly succeeding.

Prepare for frequent tips about job openings you might want to consider, delicate–and not-so-delicate–inquiries about how you're doing financially, and plenty of confusion about what you really do with all of your time. Most of the time, such comments are well-meant. Don't let those concerned folks annoy you. Just smile, tell them how much you love being your own boss and urge them to try it themselves one day. Eventually, time and your success will cure most of these concerned types of their urge to "help" you.

Even more alien to many non-Home Teamers is how a husband and wife could even consider working together in the same place. Suddenly, the first words out of the mouths of every couple you meet–even those who will swear up and down they have the best marriage you will ever see–are, "Oh, we could never work together. We're too different–we'd drive each other crazy."

"Yes, the usual reaction is, 'How can you work together without killing one another?' " says Richard Creager, who designs dolls with his wife, Jodi. "Our reply is always the same. You had better be good friends if you want to attempt it. Husband, wife, lover, sweetheart all mean nothing. In this arena, being a BEST friend means everything. You will not survive otherwise."

Michelle and Jim Foy recall getting the same reaction when they started. Through the years they have worked from home, though, they have noticed a change in the responses. "I can remember hearing that, but not recently," Jim says. "Now, people are realizing it's a better situation." Michelle adds she now detects a sense of longing in the people she talks to, and believes many of them would love to try out her lifestyle for themselves.

Another funny thing about all of those, "We're too different ... " comments is that people tend to apply that test only to spouses, not their co-workers and bosses. More often than not, people who share an office environment are wildly different from one another–and no one thinks twice about how they could work together. It's an odd comment on society's view of marriage that Home Teams are held to a different standard than other workplace teams. Every year, though, more and more couples are proving those misconceptions wrong.

And we're also out of the loop

If you want to escape the strange comments and questions upon setting up your Home Team, you can always hole up in your home office and get to work. After the first few days or weeks, though, you'll notice that won't help you evade another weird side-effect: that out-of-sorts, cut-loose feeling of having just left the somewhat predictable "real" world for a new and confusing land of shifting sands and uncertain paychecks.

While having a workplace where you set your own rules and boundaries is great, it takes some getting used to. At first, the freedom might feel less freeing than it does oppressive. You might feel like those folks from behind the Iron Curtain who rushed to the free countries of the west after their governments fell ... only to discover they couldn't deal with the dizzying array of choices they suddenly had to make every day: Where do I want to live? How do I want to earn a living? What should I study in school? Where should I buy my groceries? How should I pay–cash, check or charge? If you've grown up having to make such decisions, it's not a big deal. But if you've never faced them before, you might want to retreat back to the "safety" of your old ways, which is exactly what some of those Eastern Bloc exiles did–they went back home.

To avoid the temptation to go "back home" to a traditional office, you need to give yourself time to adjust. Even if you can set up your home office, line up a ton of work and start keeping a regular schedule in the first week, the mental transition will take longer. Sometimes, that jarring feeling will hit on that first payday when you're used to receiving a check for a certain amount and, instead, find an empty mailbox. Or maybe it will strike on an afternoon when you have no work to do and find yourself wondering, even briefly, whose permission you must ask to leave the office early.

Family business consultant Ed Hoover compares the change in thinking a new entrepreneur has to make to the feeling of graduating from college–all you've known for sixteen or more years is how to be a student, but suddenly, you aren't one anymore.

"It was an adjustment from having your lives pretty much regimented from the outside–it's a paradigm shift," Hoover says. More than just an external change in schedules or habits, it's a whole new way of looking at the world. In his case, he says, the transition took about two years after he and his wife, Colette, began working for themselves. "Now, I'm useless working for anybody else–I'm convinced of that," he says.

It's not that you really expect a paycheck every Friday, or someone else's OK before you can take a day off–it's just that you haven't figured out what you *can* expect. Is a vacation realistic in the first year? You might not know when you start out. In fact, there are some situations where you might never really know—for example, will the checks always come in steadily enough to take care of the bills? You just have to get used to uncertainty in some areas. On the plus side, though, you will find a new sense of self-control and security in other areas.

"Kenne is happy with our situation as long as there's money to pay the bills," jewelry designer Valerie Saint-Gaudens says. "When it's slow, though, he's learned not to worry. After a few years, you get used to the highs and lows, and the lows don't scare you anymore. This is important to marital health. We trust the powers that be and know that we will always have what we need. We even pray for orders together and laugh when the phone starts ringing. I guess you could say that our spirituality plays a big part in being able to do this."

Many Home Teams take similar attitudes—they say the ups and downs are much easier to take once they realize their lifestyle is the best there is.

"Actually, I feel sorry for all the folks who spend their whole lives kissing up to some boss," says Jeeni Criscenzo, an author who runs a graphics design and copywriting business from home with her partner, Joe. "When I hear someone say that they've retired after working thirty-five years for one company, I think, 'What a boring life!' I don't care how much of a pension they've got—most of their lives, they were letting someone else tell them what to do all day long."

While you're adjusting to your new-found autonomy, the quieter and less-populated home work environment also might take some getting used to. That's especially true if you've come from an office setting where a lot of people were always passing by, dropping in, calling meetings, sharing lunch and so on. It's not that you don't enjoy the company of your spouse–you're just used to having a larger and more diverse group of co-workers around you.

"The first thing that hits you is, suddenly, your contact with people is on the end of a phone," consultant Jerry Fletcher recalls. "That initially got me. A lot of my friends cannot understand how I could operate this way because they crave this person-to-person contact."

Fortunately, work-at-home types who crave more social contact can find plenty of other opportunities to get out and meet people, whether it's at chamber of commerce events, lunch meetings with clients, or business-related seminars and programs. And those who found the typical corporate office too crowded will enjoy the freedom to be alone when they need to: no more pointless staff meetings or being unexpectedly cornered at the coffee pot by the office blab.

Susan Fletcher says she's learned to appreciate the more solitary work environment. It was difficult at first, especially since she and Jerry had just moved to a new area where they didn't know anyone. But it got better and, eventually, desirable. "I just stuck it out," she says. "I'm a person who needs a certain amount of quiet. Now, it's really hard for me to imagine getting a 'real' job."

Knock, knock. Who's there?

If you crave quiet time–or even if you enjoy a lot of social interaction but also need to get your work done–there's another side-effect of working at home you have to defend against. That's the tendency of everyone from cousins to clients to next-door neighbors to think that, well, because you're at home, you must have lots of extra time to let out their dog a couple of times during the day, tape *The Price Is Right* for them, run out and pick up their kids from swim class, or just chat on the phone for an hour or so. After all, it's not as if you're really working or anything.

"Friends and family think that, when you're working at home, you have nothing to do," marketer James Patterson says. "They're on the phone bending your ear. They ask you to do things they wouldn't expect you to do if you were in an office. It takes awhile for people to take you seriously."

Jeeni Criscenzo says she and Joe must fend off interruptions all the time because of such attitudes from the non-homework crowd: "Few people understand or respect the hours I spend working and the value of my time. Joe gets upset with people who put demands on our time, because he knows how precious it is. Other people see life as working hours and free time. For us, any time could be working time if there is work to do."

Even business-related interruptions can get to be a bit much, as Sherian and Carlos Frey discovered when they opened their in-house sculpture studio. As a new and anxious Home Team, Sherian recalls, they did "about anything" to promote the fact they were still in town after leaving their teaching jobs, and offered classes at their home studio in pottery-making, macrame and other crafts up to four nights a week. The tactic drew business, she says, but it also created an unforeseen drawback.

"We were getting the traffic, but we weren't getting anything done," Sherian says. So many customers were dropping by daily, she and Carlos had no time to get any other work accomplished. Their solution was to set aside Fridays for visits from the public, and to spend the rest of the week concentrating on their sculptures. They occasionally offer other group programs during the week, but try to limit how often that happens. When they need to network and meet people, they make a point of getting out of the studio and house to visit functions sponsored by the chamber of commerce.

Personal or business-related, time-eating interruptions can be solved by setting rules that work for you ... then sticking to them. If you need eight hours of pure work time between 9 a.m. and 5 p.m.–or even just one guaranteed hour of peace and quiet every day–you need to make it clear to others they can't just drop by or expect to bend your ear on the phone during that time. If someone persists in visiting or calling, be firm and practice saying this: "I'm sorry, I'm working right now. Can I get back to you later?" And when you're hit with those errand-running requests, try a simple, "No."

The key is to help those around you understand up front that your home office is no less a workplace than your old office used to be. If someone wouldn't think of running downtown and visiting your corporate headquarters to sit at your desk, drink coffee and complain about the neighbors down the street who don't mow their lawn, then they shouldn't be doing it now that you're working at home. You don't have to be rude or crabby about it, but it's your job to make sure that message is delivered clearly.

All things come to those who ...

Finally, in getting used to your work-at-home lifestyle, be sure to arm yourself with plenty of patience and an open mind. Some matters will take longer than you expect to sort out. New skills will become a must for your business. Unforeseen challenges will arise. If you keep a realistic but healthy, positive and can-do attitude, you'll have a much better chance of both creating a successful business and enjoying the best the Home Team arrangement has to offer.

"You shouldn't go into it lightly," Margaret Hanson says. She and her husband, Bob, decided they were determined to stick through any challenges they might encounter in their embroidery business. "You have to be committed to what you're doing," she adds.

Colleen and Jerry Larson agree. "To work for yourself, you have to really, really want to," she says. You also have to be prepared to step outside your comfort zone and learn to do things you may never have done–or even thought about doing–before. Jerry, for example, found himself taking crafts classes to help move their business along. The experience was not always comfortable, partly because there were few men in the programs. On the other hand, he has learned that instruction is important for helping them achieve continued success. "I always thought I knew everything–I thought I was doing just fine without classes," he says.

Most of all, be ready to step back every so often and take a look at where you are, and where you'd like to be. Talk together about your dreams and goals, and what it will take for both of you to get there. By doing this regularly, you can make sure both of you keep moving in the right direction, at the right speed.

"In whatever you do, you have to create momentum," Renata von Tscharner says. "You're not in a company, where you can get carried along. You have to move the boat–no one else is going to do it."

And now, climb aboard the boat and weigh anchor. You've reached the point where you're ready to set sail.

The Home Team

Home Team Quiz 3: "Can You Do It?"

1) What would you do to make a Home Team business successful?
   a) I'm going to give this everything I've got, even if it means locking myself away and working from dawn to midnight seven days a week.
   b) I'll do my best. If it doesn't work out, I've got friends who can help me get a real job again.
   c) I'll help out however I can, because my spouse really wants to do this.
   d) Whatever it takes from both of us ... as long as it's legal, ethical and keeps our marriage's best interests at heart.

2) What would make you quit your Home Team attempt?
   a) Nothing. This is important to me, even if it means selling the house, car and family pets.
   b) I'd have to see. If things don't go smoothly, I might reconsider in two or three months.
   c) It's not my decision–this is my spouse's dream, so he/she must decide when enough is enough.
   d) It would have to be pretty catastrophic. Whatever happens, though, we would eventually try again because we really want to be together.

3) What would the two of you do in your business?
   a) Well, it's really my business–I've wanted to do this for a long time. But my spouse will have to help because I can't afford to hire employees.
   b) I guess we'll both do what we can and hope it works out.

Home Team Fundamentals

   c) Oh, I won't be doing any running–this is my spouse's baby, sink or swim.
   d) We haven't figured out all the details yet, but we plan to work based on what our skills, likes and dislikes are.

4) Where do you see a Home Team lifestyle taking you in ten, twenty or thirty years?
   a) I want to be rich and successful enough to buy out my old company and fire my former boss.
   b) Wherever ... we just want to do something different from what we're doing now.
   c) I just want my spouse to find something that he/she is happy with that can pay the bills.
   d) We hope to love what we do, make a positive difference in people's lives, and achieve our life's dreams.

Score:
   Did you say **a)**? It sounds as if your vision of a Home Team is just that ... your vision alone. A real team needs to plan, dream and work together.
   Was **b)** right on target? You're approaching commitment as if it's a dirty word. To make a Home Team work, you need to live and breathe commitment.
   Did **c)** best match you? Your only Home Team vision is your spouse's. You both need determination to make your partnership work.
   Was **d)** your choice? You two are on the right track–you might not have all the answers yet, but you're tackling the questions together.

Chapter 4

Your Relationship
Roles, Goals and Understanding

George Burns and Gracie Allen had a fabulous working relationship and a great marriage that stood up to both time and the infamous stresses of the entertainment industry lifestyle. There are plenty of reasons for their success at home and on the stage, but three stand out as examples for any Home Team: they had a clear picture of who they were as individuals, they knew what they wanted to achieve as a couple, and they understood each other deeply.

Clear roles, goals and understanding–couples who work at home need all three if they want their marriages and businesses to be as enjoyable and harmonious as possible.

Roles

Telling a modern Home Team to define their roles sounds at first like a politically incorrect instruction: "What do you mean?" some career women are likely to ask. "As in, 'He's the boss and I'm the assistant? No way.' " But that's not what role defining is about. It's more about deciding what balance of responsibilities works so you're each free to do your best in a comfortable environment. Think of your roles not as constraints or little mime-inspired boxes, but as personalized travel guides that steer you toward the same destination from your individual starting points. For example, if you set out from Paris by car, your partner leaves Salzburg by bicycle and you want to meet in Vienna, you're both going to need a different set of directions. But you'll both be able to enjoy the same whipped cream-filled pastries and heavenly coffee when you meet at the cafe.

Defining roles in the work-at-home world is important because no couple–no matter how close and compatible–are clones. We each have different skills, interests, experiences and ideas, so it's only natural for each of us to approach work differently. Even couples who work at the same business on the most equal of footings often gravitate toward different specialties.

"I think it's good for people to have to know themselves, be comfortable by themselves and not match the workstyle of their partner," crafter Maureen Carlson says. Some couples get too wrapped up in their individual styles, and end up criticizing the other's approach as wrong. "It has to fit with who you are," Carlson adds.

"Realize each person is an individual and not an extension of yourself," sculpture artist Colleen Larson says. "Unless it's an earth-shattering (difference), it doesn't matter."

By settling into roles, you not only will avoid head butting, but also allow your business to work more effectively. A business where he and she fall over each other every time to answer the order line, send out separate bills to the same client, or find themselves with two versions of the same business card because they both ordered supplies is a mess and an embarrassment. And it will drive customers away. Knowing who does what helps your business run smoothly and saves your sanity.

"When people get those wide-eyed, incredulous looks on their faces when we say we work together constantly, I tell how we had to find our own 'spots,' " says jewelry designer Valerie Saint-Gaudens, who runs a home business with her husband, Kenne Swink. "But this is the most important piece of information that I can give to couples who work together at home: define your jobs. Make sure you know what is expected of each of you.

"In the early days when (Kenne) was learning about gold and casting and diamonds, he would forget information. I'd get frustrated that he didn't remember in one time what I had taken years to absorb. I expected him to do tasks, and he'd be confused and think I was supposed to do them. We finally had to sit down and define our roles. Once we did that, the world was running once again in greased grooves. Very important."

Of course, it's not always easy in the early stages to know exactly what to expect from your business, much less what each of its principals will be responsible for daily. Some partners ease into roles they find they are most comfortable with.

"We didn't make any rules: you do this and I do that," recalls Eric Flaxenburg, who runs a clothing manufacturing company with his wife, Jean. "We just did the things we thought we'd do better." In their case, that meant she handled the accounting while he dealt with customers and business associates.

Define your roles as best as you can at the start, and go from there. This is not a quick-setting cement lifestyle we're talking about–you have to give it time and stay flexible. If you're not experiencing friction about who does what in the early stages, you might want to wait and see what duties you gravitate toward. On the other hand, if you start feeling unhappy with the jobs you have or sense you're always stepping on each other's toes, try talking about what you would like to do–and set more guidelines.

When you settle on your roles, remember to respect each other's primary responsibilities in the different areas. This doesn't mean you can't suggest a new sales strategy to a husband who's the de facto marketing director of your publishing business while you handle development. Not at all–you need to keep communication as open and freely flowing as possible. It does mean, though, that you should avoid second-guessing your husband's every move if you agreed to relinquish the marketing decisions. Let him do his job and expect that he will let you do yours.

Jeeni Criscenzo, who runs a graphics design and copywriting business with her partner, Joe, acknowledges this area was a challenge for them. She says she drives Joe crazy by cleaning her office when she's in the middle of a project–to her, it's creative thinking time; to him, it's a waste of time. They've come to realize, though, that their differences stem from their separate roles: she's the creative talent who fuels the business, he's the business manager who keeps it profitable.

"I don't take things as seriously as him," she says. "I consistently underbid projects–I have a hard time asking people for money for things that come easily to me and that I enjoy doing. But then I'm miserable when I don't have enough money and I've been working night and day. So I've learned to let Joe handle the pricing, and he's learned to leave me alone when he sees me doing my organizing rituals."

Whether you spell out roles from president to janitor, or start out by developing rough guidelines and easing into duties, it is vital that you decide quickly who is going to make the final decisions on matters. We hope you already decided this during the business plan exercises in the last chapter. Everything is dandy when you see eye to eye. But when you have major differences of opinion–and you will have plenty–what will you do to come up with a solution that helps the businesses and leaves you both satisfied?

Even if you run separate businesses, or have set up an employer-employee working relationship, decisions come up that affect the family finances. And, when you work as full partners, what do you do when you stand in opposite corners on a decision that affects you both equally?

While each situation is unique, we have found this to be true in most cases: While all important decisions must be discussed, ONE OF YOU must be empowered to make the final call on business matters.

Where you go from there is up to you. When there are disagreements, start by trying to compromise. You might find an even better solution than you previously considered. But other times, compromise ends up resembling what you reap from politics. And that's not always pretty or desirable when the result hurts business, your relationship or both–either because of inaction or going with an inferior choice that satisfied both of you to a small degree.

Couples deal with this in a variety of ways. Some stick to a strict employer-employee relationship. Others do that, but switch roles every so often. Other Home Teams divide business duties, and make decisions based on who heads what area. Whatever is best for you, develop a system for resolving disagreements. And fight the temptation of playing to win during disputes. Do what is best for both the businesses and your relationship.

Figure out where you're going ... together

If you're making the commitment to work together, you need to be prepared to commit together ... and for the long haul. Long-term ventures have a much better chance of success when they are accompanied by long-term goals, so be ready to spend time talking with your spouse and planning your future–both business and personal. We hope you already took the time to do so while reading the last chapter.

Working as a Home Team is more rewarding if you have a clear picture of what you're both working toward, and how to get there. Think of it as the biggest family vacation you've ever taken: you're not just going to get in the car and drive. You'll want to arm yourselves with maps, travel guides, gas money, hotel reservations, credit cards ... maybe even some aspirin. And you'll need to know where you're heading, otherwise you could find yourselves driving in circles for the rest of your lives.

Goal setting is an important part of Jo Lutnes' household routine. She and her husband, Keith, usually assess their short-term goals monthly and go over their intermediate goals every six months to a year. They also try to stay focused on longer-term goals, such as buying a larger property for their organic farming business.

"I've got my next two businesses planned," she says–a bookstore and a consignment business are both dreams for the future. Another goal is to have Keith at home more often–he was traveling seven months one year–once they have a larger plot of land to farm.

Sometimes, life is leftover king crab legs. Other times, it is more like what you find hiding behind the pickles in the back corner of the refrigerator–messy and full of surprises. Changes in plans are guaranteed, both out of evolving needs and wants, and out of unexpected necessity. That's why it's so important for Home Teams to communicate their objectives regularly. And if you find yourselves disagreeing about where you want to go, talk matters out until you find common ground.

This is true even if you're running separate businesses. No matter how different your work is, you're still a partnership. You share a home and a marriage, and you want to make sure it stays that way. So make sure whatever you do as a Home Team is good for both. Agreeing on goals might take long, even agonizing talks, but that's OK. Because not talking things out could damage both your businesses and relationship. Just make sure, as partners in any good marriage do, that it's not always the same person doing all the giving while the other does all the taking.

"Ellie and I are in a joint venture, each as CEO of our own division, and consultants to each other," says cowboy-poet Ham Hamilton, who runs a publishing business from his Idaho home with his wife. "We speak freely about how things can be more easily accomplished, about goals, and calendar in regular sessions, and we each expect to do our share."

Rather than viewing every issue in black and white, consultants Michelle and Jim Foy have learned to work at finding a middle ground they can live with. "His reality and my reality are different," she says. "We negotiate an awful lot. Our conflicts are few and silly. We've learned a lot."

As your goals evolve, also make sure you're both in on the process. A healthy Home Team doesn't make unilateral decisions about major business changes or spring surprises on each other. Focusing on where you're going is only part of the game–the two of you also need to share the same focal point. You have to keep communicating to make sure that happens.

"Clear channels of communication are important," says Renata von Tscharner, who handles the daily planning for the business she runs with her husband, Ronald Lee Fleming. "We even write memos to each other to make sure we're clear. We each have calendars that routinize things. Weekly codes explain where we are every hour of the day."

Doll-maker Richard Creager says: "We set goals together both in business and personal matters. We try to function as a team whenever we work on establishing any decisions which affect our common future. When you have been working together as long as we have, it feels unnatural not to consult one another."

In all your planning and talking, remember to keep your relationship a high priority. The marriage must be prioritized above the businesses, above the kids, above all else but your faith.

Promise yourselves that, if you ever believe your business is hurting your marriage, you will step back and direct all of your energies toward solving the personal problems. Reorganizing your work, starting a different business, taking on a temporary outside job to see your business through a hard time–these are all easier than the pain of having to start your lives over again because the marriage was neglected. Never let work become a damaging influence on your relationship. Always remember what is truly important.

As family business consultants, Colette and Ed Hoover have seen plenty of family battles that were rooted in business problems. Fights might erupt over the line of succession after the company's founder retires or dies. Or siblings with equal holdings in a firm might lock horns over what sort of business investments to make, or salaries to collect. Or spouses might clash when one wants to take on a risky new enterprise and the other doesn't. Whatever the cause, when business challenges become personal, families can be badly hurt. On the other hand, if a company's problems can be solved, relationships tend to improve.

Remember that setting goals helps keep you motivated through the daily ups and downs of running a business and a home. A thousand and one little things can sap your energy during an average day. The big picture–why you're doing this to begin with–starts getting buried. And, pretty soon, the little stuff is all you're thinking about. You don't want that to happen.

"Your marriage is a business," cowboy-poet Ham Hamilton says. "Two people gathering assets, influencing others, establishing a territory, leaving a legacy. Where and when and how you do all this is a joint decision. Don't let unimportant junk accumulate, nor junk thought predominate, wherever or however you go for your golden years." His solution is to "pray always, jointly and severally, fervently and faithfully, gratefully and hopefully."

Dan Carlson, who runs the mail-order side of a sculpture and modeling compound business, agrees a healthy perspective is important: "We each have our own goals, and we do take time to discuss them often—expanding our business, trips we want to take, money we want to make so we can get away more often. We are enjoying the opportunities we have in our home business, because one never knows what each day will bring."

Keeping your eyes on your goals should be something you strive for, even though it's not always easy to meet your expectations.

"Kenne and I have planning sessions often," jewelry designer Valerie Saint-Gaudens says. "We do our best in the car driving the half-hour to town. The challenge is to remember our best-laid plans and carry them through. In the course of daily business, the bigger plans get postponed. Then we wake up and say, 'That was such a good idea, why didn't we do it?' Well, it's time, basically. We are a two-man show, and it's hard to be everything."

Most Home Teams face a similar hurdle: there's always too much to do and never enough time. But don't allow that to make you lose sight of your dreams. To be sure you're steadily moving in the right direction, you have to find some way to keep the big picture in front of you. If your goal is to retire in ten years, write that down on a sticky note and keep it in your calendar where you can see it every day. If you want to earn enough money for a four-bedroom house in the country, find a picture of your dream home and hang it on your office wall by the computer. Whatever it takes to keep your goals in front of you, do it.

Speaking of inspiration, don't forget to keep a picture of the spouse and kids on your desk. You will be more inspired in your daily work, no matter how mundane it might seem sometimes. And you'll make sure that at least a few of those thousand and one little things every day are helping you move toward your long-term dreams.

Any goal worth working toward will take time and patience, but what other choice do you have? The last time we checked, you had to work in the laboratory at least a few years before expecting to win a Nobel Prize for physics. Consider the perspective of Jeff Ball, who with his ex-wife, Liz, has turned the concept of "yardening"–yard care for non-gardeners–into a two-person industry and is finally beginning to see years of effort pay off: "We're going to be those overnight sensations that took only twelve years to get ready," he says. For most of us, "overnight" success will require the same kind of work and time. But the odds of a payoff in the end will be better than you will ever get playing Lotto or Powerball.

Understanding

Topping the list of important qualities for any Home Team is understanding: realizing that your partner's thoughts, feelings, interests and desires are at least as important as your own and are worth knowing–and responding to–as well as you can.

A healthy level of understanding requires you to realize you are both individuals with different backgrounds, influences and perceptions. The same situations or experiences can have different meanings to both of you–not because one is right and the other is foolish, but because you have different styles of viewing and dealing with the world. Understanding why these differences exist–and how they might manifest themselves while you're working together–can help a Home Team avoid a lot of unnecessary troubles.

Understanding differences

There are more books out there than we care to count that focus on the differences between men and women. Well, no kidding, men and women are different. But so are any two people of the same sex, even identical twins.

The key as a Home Team is not to generalize each other's differences–"Oh, you men are all alike" or "Why are you women always doing that?"–but to understand each other as individuals. Stereotypes can be dangerous. How else would you account for all the marriages out there where she's the money manager while he prefers doing the laundry, or where he goes bananas whenever he sees a baby while she finds it more exciting to look at powerboats?

In one Home Team household we encountered, for example, he handles most of the cooking because he enjoys it. They've settled on their individual responsibilities, both personal and work-related. It's not that they don't have their differences, it's just that they understand each other when the differences become an issue and work to overcome obstacles.

"(My wife's) need for social interaction, and susceptibility to mood swings and cabin fever sometimes makes life difficult for me," he says. "I look at all the bills and the need to get work done to earn the money to pay for the things we like, and have difficulty with her desire to stop and get out. On the other hand, I am generally an optimist and refuse to let too many things worry me for too long. I don't crave social intercourse and am perfectly content to spend long hours working, largely because I enjoy what I do. I rarely get cabin fever and don't think I have mood swings.

"Of course, the question is, how does this affect our relationship," he continues. "Not at all. Momentary frustration is about all that it amounts to. I wouldn't be so happy with (her) if she were a carbon copy of me. I'd be bored. We deal with these differences by discussion and compromise."

One important factor in understanding each other is to understand yourself first ... then make sure your spouse knows where you're coming from. So, first, think about the things that annoy you, amuse you, stimulate you, frighten you, sadden you and bore you and, second, make sure you explain clearly to your partner what makes you feel certain ways and why.

For example, if you get irritated when someone interrupts you while you're deep in thought, you had better realize that you're the type who needs time when you're assured of being left alone. And you had better make it clear to your spouse that, nothing personal, "I just need to be lost in thought sometimes, so I'll close my office door when I feel that way. Office door open, come on in. Office door shut, I'm in the middle of major meditation and will lose my mind if disturbed."

Understanding your feelings and reactions also is important when you are discussing, debating or planning anything. Remember one piece of advice marriage counselors frequently give their clients: rather than act as an accuser and tell a spouse, "You make me so mad when you ... ," it's more constructive to say, "You know, I feel really angry whenever ... happens." This not only takes unnecessary heat out of a conversation, but reduces the temptation for your spouse to turn defensive. The only way you can use the "I feel" approach, though, is to know first what you feel and why. So take a long look at yourself before trying to get into your partner's head.

That brings us to the next, and even more difficult, step: understanding your spouse. No one can really know what is going on in another person's mind and heart at all times, but if you plan on living with someone for fifty-plus years–much less working with that person–it sure helps to try.

Understanding your spouse means more than hearing the words he or she says and figuring out the meaning. The Random House dictionary gives fourteen definitions of the word "understand," including: "to be thoroughly familiar with; apprehend clearly the character, nature, or subtleties of," "to grasp the significance, implications, or importance of," and "to accept tolerantly or sympathetically." Every one of these meanings of the word must be put to the test.

Of course, the best way to grasp, accept and understand what makes your spouse tick is for the two of you to talk ... frequently, openly and in depth. Talk about what you enjoy most about each other. Talk about your insecurities. Talk about what you'd like to achieve with your work. Make sure you regularly have a quiet and relaxing time when the two of you can get together and discuss whatever is on your minds. Make these times something to look forward to: maybe a late Saturday night spent chatting on the couch in front of a cozy fire, or a leisurely Sunday afternoon over cappuccino and biscotti at the local cafe. Even after years together, a couple can learn surprising facts about each other by taking the time to open up.

"We hold business discussions in the car, in the kitchen," says Aron Shtull-Trauring, who works with his wife, Simcha. Talking is the best way to eliminate conflict, he says, and because they're together so much, finding time for discussions is both convenient and time-efficient. However, he adds one note of caution: "We try to avoid business discussions in the shower." There's one other place you should avoid talking shop: the bedroom. If work must spill over, physically and mentally, into all other areas of the home, at least keep it out of the bedroom. Let that be your special retreat.

Maureen Carlson says the most important factor that has allowed her and her husband, Dan, to work together is "the ability to sit down and hammer it out, talk about things that are bothering me. I tend to carry work problems with me into my personal day. He can turn it off. I think men are more used to confrontation." Facing those feelings head-on by talking about them helps clear the air for both. By taking time to discuss concerns, Home Teams can prevent nagging little problems from ballooning.

Armed with experience and knowledge of how your spouse thinks and operates, you're in a better position to manage your businesses in the most effective way possible. When he suddenly is silent while you are discussing your current advertising campaign, you'll know it is possible that something is bothering him and will work to draw out his concerns. And if she starts bouncing into your office every three minutes and interrupting you with assorted trivial questions and comments, you'll know she might have something else on her mind that she's dying to tell you ... but won't until you're ready to take a break. By understanding each other, you'll know not to get angry at such unexpected silences or interruptions, but to ask questions about what's *really* going on in your partner's head.

On the other hand, you also need to understand each other enough to know when to take a timeout. Maybe you're feeling hot under the collar and ready to pop the next time someone–and it's likely to be your spouse–approaches you with a comment of any kind. Know when you're feeling like that and warn your spouse that you need to be left alone for a bit. Nothing personal, but you just need to cool off before talking about anything. And if you're in the middle of a business discussion that snowballs into a personal argument, know enough to step back and coolly assess what the real concern is, rather than going on the attack or the defensive.

Couples who work together "really know how to get to each other," family business consultant Ed Hoover says. "You personalize the business problems in the other person. We really had to work hard at timeout.

"One device we use with family businesses and ourselves is to slow down the conversation," he adds. When a discussion heats up, stop yourselves and take a look at what you're really saying to each other, and wait before saying anything more. This approach not only helps foster understanding, but reduces the risk of a work disagreement turning into a nasty and hurtful dispute that you'll end up taking to bed with each other (or to the couch, alone) for days or weeks to come.

Understanding is more than a defensive weapon for avoiding arguments, though. It's a positive tool for nurturing a healthy relationship and making sure it continues to grow. The key here is to acknowledge your spouse as an independent person with needs of her own, not as an appendage of yourself. Remembering this, you'll know to treat your spouse as you would want to be treated: with encouragement, empathy, respect and, of course, love. And you'll avoid the temptation of trying to push your partner into doing or being something he doesn't want.

It sometimes feels as if you need to be a mind-reader to achieve this, but this is the type of treatment we all need. To be told, "Go for it," when we need a little confidence boosting. To be told, "I'm sorry, I understand," when something goes wrong. To be told, "I love you–you're the best," at just about any time.

A Home Team needs "patience, tolerance of differences, encouragement, 'respectful' fights and frequent pats on the back–the same ingredients you might put into a good marriage," Simcha Shtull-Trauring says. "Most recipes, I cut back on everything–you know, oh ever-slim lady readers: half the oil, half the sugar, half the taste. In this case, pour it on thick."

Carolyn Edlund echoes that advice:

"I've read *so* many books on the subject (of relationships)," says Carolyn, who shares a home, publishing business and freelance editorial service with her partner, Richard Adin. Her conclusion? "Just be upfront with each other. Communicate, communicate, communicate–this cannot be overemphasized. Be kind to each other. Gives lots of hugs and kisses. Express your mutual affection every day–several times each day. Compliment each other on appearance. Help each other–often, with everything. Be open-minded. Give each other some space–we all need some privacy."

Susan Schandel, who shares an accounting business with her husband, Terry, says: "We have changed. It was not perfect in the beginning, but you have to be able to see things through the other person's eyes."

Understanding challenges

No matter how ideal any situation might be, it's never perfect. To some, Hawaii is the most beautiful place in the world: mild temperatures year-round, beautiful beaches, great food and drinks ... but it's still prone to the occasional hurricane, experiences crime as does any other part of the world, and can be a pricey place to live. And some thirty-five-year-olds might believe their age is the perfect chronological condition: they've escaped the insecurities of the teens and twenties, know what they want to do with their lives and are well on their way. But, physically, they're not as resilient as a seventeen-year-old–as any thirty-ish guy has learned while trying to play basketball as he used to–and they're probably not as wise, serene and experienced as a happy, healthy sixty-eight-year-old.

So nothing's perfect, right? That might not be the biggest revelation you will experience today, but it's important to remember when you're entering the Home Team world. Understanding that the lifestyle has its ups and downs is the best way to ensure you'll have a satisfying, rewarding time living and working together in the years and decades to come.

During the first two years of their business, Colette and Ed Hoover found much of their time was eaten by the need to find clients and get out and market their business. "Those were very difficult years, stressful on our relationship, stressful on our psyches, stressful on our daughter. ... Anyone going into business needs to open up their eyes and not expect Easy Street," Colette says.

Disagreements and anger can pop up frequently during such times of stress. As a committed Home Team, you can't expect to avoid them–you just have to learn to resolve them in a constructive way.

"If we disagree about something, we just hash it out until we come to an agreement–sometimes at a few decibels higher than necessary, but at least things don't fester the way they did in other relationships," Jeeni Criscenzo says. "We can't afford to be angry for long because it will cost us money. If I'm upset, I can't be creative. If Joe is upset, it makes me upset. So we've learned to get things out and get over it."

Maybe an issue will arise over which the two of you just can't agree. What do you do then? Depending upon the type of business you run, maybe you can each do your own thing on this particular matter. For example, if you create one-of-a-kind rugs together and each have a separate vision for your latest design, you might find it more rewarding to craft two versions.

On the other hand, this solution is less likely to work if you prepare tax documents for small businesses or run a real estate business together—it's probably not the best of ideas to hand a client two versions of a tax return or suggest two different list prices for a home. If the do-your-own-thing solution won't work, one of you might just have to swallow your objections and give in this time. It's not necessarily the most satisfying agreement, but make sure you reach it with a smile. There are few things more frustrating than a Home Team partner who carries a grudge. No, "I told you so's," either.

Publishers and editors Rich Adin and Carolyn Edlund say they have learned to resolve work disputes by giving in to the partner with the most experience in the area of conflict.

"Our work and home environment is quite egalitarian," Adin says. "We may argue a little about something, but it is very little and the ultimate decision-making is deferred to the person with the most expertise. For example, when we do a book cover design, Carolyn is the artist. I give input primarily from the marketing perspective, but ultimate artistic control is given to Carolyn. We tend to make the decisions jointly by default with that subconscious weighing of the expertise factor."

Another important key is that no one knows everything, so don't fall into the trap of thinking you're always right in a disagreement, or believe you can do everything in your business without help. The beauty of sharing a home and a working relationship is that there are two of you to balance out each other's limitations—and everyone has them. It takes practice to learn to be humble, but if you can acquire this skill, you'll be a lot happier working together—and probably more successful. By listening to your partner, rather than insisting you're right, you might actually learn something that will benefit your business. And, even if you are right, you still can benefit from carefully considering perspectives, ideas and concerns other than your own.

"When you're both stubborn ... you have to be able to admit you made a mistake," embroidery business owner Margaret Hanson says.

In Bob Pettingell's case, his wife Charlene's concerns about the money he was investing to start an annual jazz festival began dissolving as she became caught up in the work. "My wife was very worried that we'd end up spending our money," he says. Despite that debt, though, "She's caught up in it now. She's come to see what an exciting thing this is."

Remember that rough spots–in marriage and business–aren't necessarily portents of doom. Handled with determination, understanding and an open mind, challenges will help you grow, personally and professionally. It's not always pleasant, but you'll both be better people for it.

Finally, keep your eye on the big picture–that is, your relationship and how you want it to be. No matter what disagreements you might have, no matter what challenges you encounter, no matter how frustrated or steamed your spouse might make you feel sometimes, keep in mind the good things about each other. Think back to your first date, your favorite weekend activity, your shared interests, your love for each other. That will help you through the moments of unpleasantness during what should–and can–be a romantic, lifelong Home Team cruise.

"You've got to love working at home, be OK with the ups and downs of self-employment and get adjusted to each other's way of dealing with those ups and downs," says Diane Pfeifer Justice, an author who works with her husband, Jeff. "Be supportive but realistic."

Understanding benefits

Most of all, it helps if you're both convinced you've chosen the best possible way of living and working. You can be there for each other to cheer during the good days and comfort during the bad, to give unconditional inspiration and encouragement, to do what no other co-worker can do, and to provide what solo entrepreneurship can't offer. Have faith in each other and the mission you have chosen, proceed with confidence and have fun. Whenever you reach a hurdle, just remind yourself of that, take a deep breath and jump. You'll make it ... together.

Now, about those hurdles—let's look at those next.

THE HOME TEAM

Home Team Quiz 4: "How's Your Teamwork?"

1) How do you resolve disagreements?
   a) We argue until one wins and the other loses.
   b) Most things aren't worth fighting about–I just let my spouse handle most issues.
   c) We don't argue–if we disagree with each other, we try to keep it to ourselves.
   d) We talk and try to understand each other's point of view. We usually compromise, but neither of us is afraid to admit being wrong.

2) How do you tackle big projects together–such as redecorating, shopping for a car, or planning a party?
   a) Together? We'd probably kill each other. I control the house stuff while my spouse handles anything business- or financial-related.
   b) I try to not get too wrapped up in stuff like that–my spouse is happy handling things alone.
   c) We just jump in and hope for the best–sometimes it works, sometimes we end up giving each other the silent treatment for a few days.
   d) We do a lot of talking first to make sure we're on the same page. Hashing things out can take awhile, but we're usually happy with the results.

3) What do you two like to do for fun?
   a) I like sports, but I hate playing with my spouse because he/she isn't very good. He/she enjoys seeing plays, but you couldn't drag me to one.
   b) I like to go out with my friends, and my spouse likes to goof around on the computer. We don't do much together–our tastes are too different.

Your Relationship

c) We go out to eat pretty often. I'd like to do something different once–maybe visit a museum or go sailing. I don't think my spouse would care for that, though, so I don't try to change things.

d) We enjoy being with each other, so almost anything can be fun. We share a lot of interests, and always look out for new things to try.

4) How do you share household responsibilities?
   a) Share? I do everything, even though it's never to my spouse's satisfaction.
   b) I take care of things if they start driving me crazy, and my spouse does the same.
   c) I know my spouse means well, but I end up doing everything over again when he/she "helps" with dishes, yardwork, etc. He/she just doesn't do it the right way.
   d) We try to carry an equal load, with the work divided according to our likes and dislikes.

Score:

Was **a)** your choice? Sounds as if you each try to nab the whole cookie jar instead of sharing. Home Teams need negotiation, not winners and losers.

Did **b)** sound most like you? Laissez faire doesn't work here. You need to put more effort and caring–together–into a Home Team to make it work.

Did you say **c)**? Hey, it's OK to disagree–it's just how you express your feelings. Get used to compromise and discussing differences if you want to be a Home Team.

Was the best match **d)**? You seem to have the hang of the teamwork thing. Keep it up!

Chapter 5
Slobs vs. Neat Freaks (and Other Challenges)

Felix Unger and Oscar Madison had it easy: they had to share only an apartment. Imagine if they had to share an office, too.

The Battle of Styles is a harsh reality, not a sitcom, for work-at-home couples. He needs his office supplies arranged in alphabetical order on the desk before he can sit down at the computer; she works best from a small open spot on the floor surrounded by stacks of files, news clippings, books and used coffee cups. When these offices are in the same home–or trickier yet, when couples share an office–married life can get, ummmm, interesting.

Consider Alex and Meera Censor. He's a computer consultant and writer; she's a massage therapist, portrait sculptor and transcriber. And they work together in a four-hundred-fifty-square-foot house in San Diego. He runs his businesses from a corner of the living room, and she operates out of a nook seventeen feet away. "Sometimes, there's tension about whose space is what," Alex says. "My stuff tends to accumulate in piles. Meera has a real need for harmony."

Complicating their clash of organizational styles is Alex's work as a computer software reviewer. Publicity packages arrive daily, and they pile up fast. With the Censors' limited room, shelf space is at a premium. Meera has, on occasion, had to battle for her fair share. Once, she stalked through their work area with a ruler to measure who was using more shelf space. Space isn't the only concern, either: the condition of Alex's office area also can raise Meera's hackles. "There's kind of a tension about, 'When are you going to clean up your desk?'" he acknowledges.

The Censors aren't alone: the battle of meticulous vs. messy is one of the most common–and most heated–complaints of work-at-home couples. Here is another case where, hackneyed as it sounds, it's often true that opposites attract: "There's always tension on that front," says Ronald Lee Fleming, who runs a planning organization with his wife, Renata von Tscharner. "Because of our strong personalities, we think there will always be someone else to clean up the mess. If no one does the filing, it will grow out of control. In my case, that's a major grievance. It hurts my effectiveness."

Renata says it's not that she doesn't want things neat and tidy–it's just that working at home and caring for children means housekeeping sometimes has to take the back seat. There's not always enough time to be Mrs. Clean.

The clutter conflict

The above situation illustrates a common, two-fold problem for couples who work at home.

First, the dual office means no more hiding organizational idiosyncrasies in a workplace miles away. If his old desk downtown resembled ground zero, but she saw it only on those rare occasions when she met him for lunch, it was no big deal. But if she has to walk past a federal disaster area in her own home every time she heads to the bathroom or steps out for a cup of coffee, it becomes harder to ignore.

Second, work-at-home couples usually are surprised by how quickly their businesses overwhelm the home, both in time and space. Not only is it difficult to keep the offices neat, but finding the time to clean the rest of the house becomes an even greater challenge. All those hours saved commuting don't necessarily translate into more time for housecleaning–probably because, given the choice between finishing a project that will result in a two-thousand-five-hundred-dollar check or finishing the laundry, most people will say, "Hey, these socks don't smell yet."

The solutions to this two-headed challenge are as varied as the couples themselves. For some, separate workspaces can ease the tensions of the "Odd Couple" office. That way, all Fussy has to do is look at Scruffy's mess, not work in it. Individual desks or work areas are pretty much a necessity anyway–even if a couple shares the same business and duties, both need spaces to call their own. "In the same home is all right," consultant Jerry Fletcher says. "In the same room would be an absolute disaster."

Not all couples feel that way. There are plenty who share office space and say the arrangement isn't anything close to a day at Krakatoa. However, even they agree that seismograph needles would zig-zag wildly if each partner couldn't stake claim to at least some workspace–even if it's just a desktop and one file drawer–to call his or her own.

One of the first things Colleen and Jerry Larson did when they started their sculpture business was to buy separate desks. It worked out well, Colleen says, "because Jerry is more organized than I am." The rest of the house is a separate battlefield, though–she wants it more tidy than he does.

Jewelry designer Valerie Saint-Gaudens says a significant amount of early tension disappeared when she and her husband, Kenne Swink, learned to demarcate their work spaces.

"We joke about an invisible line down the center of our office dividing his computer and 'shipping department' from my desk and jeweler's bench," she says.

Time–and a willingness to compromise–also can help even out the differences. "When we started, I was fastidious about files and records," says Terry Schandel, who has shared a CPA business with his wife since 1978. "It wasn't that important to Susan. So we met in the middle. We do things the same now–we found a middle ground."

When worlds collide

For some, though, the war of clean versus chaos is ongoing. He can't ignore her desktop mess because they must exchange papers, reports and files a dozen times a day–and he can never relocate anything once he has handed it to her. Or she finds it hard to overlook the stacks of ancient *Time* magazines on the floor beside his table because she keeps tripping over them to get to her desk. When that happens, it might help to bring in a mediator of sorts–that is, a professional organizer or space planner.

"A lot of times, people call me when they're in pain," professional organizer Thalia Poulos says. A couple's lack of order could be hurting their work–maybe they can't find their insurance records, or they're under-billing because they aren't keeping accurate track of their hours. Or the work stresses might already have dug deeper and started to hurt their relationship.

When Poulos steps in to help a work-at-home couple, she encourages them to agree to a few guidelines about their workspace. First, she says, settle on which parts of your home will make up the "safety zone"–common areas such as the bedroom, bathroom, kitchen and family room that you will keep up to mutually acceptable standards. It doesn't matter if you're the ultimate pack rat and your partner is fanatical about keeping every countertop, table and shelf one-hundred-percent clutter-free. You will have to compromise on what your safety zone should look like, then make sure it stays that way.

The safety zone approach also eliminates the potential for territorial disputes. By agreeing on which areas are shared, you'll know which rooms you can walk into freely at all times without encountering icy stares from your hard-at-work partner who does not want to be disturbed.

This solution worked for Mark and Susan Detwiler. They say placing the computer and modem in their safety zone eliminated problems they used to encounter before they became a Home Team. When Susan worked outside the home, she found it annoying when Mark stopped in to use the office equipment. "It was almost like he was invading my turf," she says. With the office equipment now on neutral ground, she no longer feels that way.

After settling on your safety zone, you need to agree upon a personal space for each of you. "You can each have one room where you can do whatever you will," Poulos says. If you don't have separate rooms, map out which portion of your shared office will be off limits. And no matter how high the junk piles in that area, or how anally alphabetized the supplies and files are, the other person is not allowed to say anything, Poulos advises. His office is his. Hers is hers. Case closed.

This is the solution we reached to solve a nagging problem. Shirley has a fear that someday, she's certain she will need those stacks of decade-old plan commission meeting minutes for reference. Scott, on the other hand, sometimes acts as if he missed his calling to work on a recycling truck. We decided we would allow each other to do whatever we wanted with our separate offices–not that we have to like it, just keep our mouths zipped about it. As the years have gone by, we've moved more toward center on our definition

Slobs vs. Neat Freaks

of clutter. This will allow us, we hope, to work together in one office someday.

If you're both in the same business, there might be times when you need to share resources. If that's the case, you'll have to settle on a storage system that works for both of you, even if you're on opposite ends of the organizing spectrum.

That might sound impossible, but it can be done. First, each of you should identify what type of organizing strategy works best. Do you tend to keep current projects on the desk where you can keep an eye on them, rather than file them away? Or do you like to put everything in its place the moment you've finished work for the day? Do you have a hard time throwing things away? Or are you brutal with clutter, with every piece of paper you toss representing a small, personal victory? Are you a stacker? Or do you have no organizing system at all?

Once you know what kind of organizers you are, you can combine systems to create an arrangement that works well for both. How do you do that? "Look at who needs what, and give them what they need," Poulos says.

For example, maybe you have to have everything neatly put away as soon as you've completed a project, and your spouse needs to see with one glance where all her resources are. You can blend your styles by storing all of your mutual papers in a lateral file cabinet–Poulos prefers these over the usual vertical file drawers–with big labels on every folder and on the outside of the drawer. That way, you have everything in its place, and your spouse can identify instantly by the labels where the papers she needs are kept.

Part of the difference in how people organize comes from how they make decisions. Think about how you open your mail. A quick decision-maker likes to settle right away what goes in the garbage or recycling bin, what needs to be answered or paid, and what can be filed away for future use. A more deliberate decision-maker, on the other hand, likes to keep her options open. She will want to keep some of the mail that he would rather throw out. Not because she needs it or has a specific use in mind–it just might come in handy some day. "I think that shows at their desks," Poulos says. "I see it all the time when I work with couples."

The way to resolve those differences when handling mutual tasks is to establish rituals. "I do, 'Same time, same place,' " Poulos says. That means, for example, always opening the mail in the kitchen right after dinner, or wherever and whenever it's convenient for both. No more dragging some pieces into the basement while you use the treadmill, or tucking mail under the flower pot until you've decided what to do with it.

You also should settle on a plan of attack that doesn't saddle either of you with duties you hate. If you like answering mail and your spouse prefers handling the checkbook, you should take over the letter-writing duties while your honey pays the bills–all at the appointed times and places. "Who's going to do it? Figure out your strengths and use teamwork," Poulos recommends.

Working with a professional organizer made a big difference for Brad and Rosemarie Barbeau, a Chicago couple who turned to Poulos for help in improving the efficiency of their shared apartment office. In their case, it wasn't so much organizing differences that were causing problems. It was mainly a lack of storage space.

"We both just made piles," says Brad, a faculty member at the University of Chicago who works at home several evenings a week. Their two filing cabinets were full and not very accessible. Both he and Rosemarie were overwhelmed by paper.

Besides adding a new cabinet to their office, the Barbeaus built a set of shelves into the room's closet, a move that added a significant amount of storage. They also made two other changes: adding a second phone line for those times when Brad and Rosemarie–a full-time, home-based consultant in team-building for organizations–both worked in their office simultaneously; and finding a professional to handle their personal and business bills, a job Brad found was eating too much of his time.

As beneficial as those changes have been, a commitment to stick to them also is important: "I still make piles," Brad says. "Paper still comes in faster than I can get rid of it. If I start to get behind on that, the system starts to fall apart."

But who's going to wash the dog?

What about the mess outside of the offices? How can couples avoid butting heads over who does the laundry, who scrubs the greasy dinner skillets and who is responsible for shuttling little Katie to her twice-a-week, after-school gymnastics practices?

In some work-at-home households, tradition reigns: while both husband and wife share business duties, she also takes care of most of the shopping, cooking and housekeeping, while he shoulders more professional responsibilities.

Carolyn Sherman works with her husband, Bob, at two businesses–a news service and an information brokerage–but also handles all the household chores. Carolyn often doesn't get to bed until 1 or 1:30 in the morning, and usually wakes up at 6 or 7 when the Great Dane realizes it's daybreak. For the Shermans, it's a system that has worked well for many years and allowed them to enjoy what they consider the important things in life: each other and their son. As Bob says, they enjoy "one hell of a marriage."

Many other couples, though, share the chores that confront them outside their office doors. The goal often isn't a straight-down-the-middle split, but a balance of chores based on schedules, or simply who dislikes doing what the

THE HOME TEAM

least. For quite a few Home Teams, this approach satisfies both partners.

Management consultants Michelle and Jim Foy negotiated a trade after they started working together: he agreed to handle the laundry if she would take over the household finances. Before, he'd always been the one to balance the checkbook and pay the family bills, but he hated it–it was too similar to what he'd done for a living in the audit department of a cosmetics company. On the other hand, she despised cleaning clothes. So they both concluded it made sense to switch. "We merrily went on our way and have done so ever since," Jim says.

Jim adds he enjoys doing the laundry, because it's a job with a clear beginning and end. He says it also helps his work when he takes a break in the middle of the day to throw a few loads of dirty clothes into the washer–he's not at his desk, but he can keep thinking about the day's project while accomplishing something else. Michelle says the trade helped break down the barriers that existed around chores in their household. Jim now does the vacuuming, also, while she reigns in the kitchen.

Susan and Jerry Fletcher–she's a writer, he's in direct marketing–also have struck a balance. He washes the dishes after dinner, and usually spends part of the morning straightening up the kitchen and family room. Susan handles dinner and laundry. "I'm laundry illiterate," Jerry says. "By choice," Susan pipes in.

Getting used to a new balance of chores took Susan awhile. The first week Jerry joined her at home, she'd offer to make lunch for them both. The result: he left all the dishes for her to clean. She doesn't do that anymore–both take care of their own lunches–but the current solution is still less than perfect: "Now we're both kind of bad about the lunch dishes," she acknowledges.

Slobs vs. Neat Freaks

Other Home Team couples find themselves in a similar situation: no matter how carefully they plot the division of labor, certain jobs fall to the bottom of the priority list. Laundering, grocery shopping and, yes, even dishwashing are unavoidable–you can let the sink and hamper fill only so high, or the refrigerator contents dwindle only so much before there is nothing left to wear, nothing left to eat and nothing left to eat off of. But dusting? Vacuuming? Making the bed? Sorting through that stack of old newspapers growing behind the couch? It's easy to put those off for a long time, even though the results can drive some couples crazy.

For some, the solution is outside help. Even if it's only once every two weeks or once a month, calling in an extra pair of hands to tidy up can save a lot of aggravation.

Colleen and Jerry Larson hired someone to clean their house when they started traveling to Minnesota's Renaissance Fair in the summers to display and sell their fantasy-inspired sculptures. They plan to use cleaning help again in coming seasons because their busy summer schedule leaves little time for anything but work.

Maids used to be a luxury. Today, they can be a smart business decision. Follow the advice printed on a flyer a cleaning woman once stuck on our door handle: "Do you want your home clean, like in a fairy tale? Yes, it's possible even in this recession!" Hey, she can't write ad copy and we can't clean, so it all evens out.

For those who are thinking, "I can't afford a maid," ask yourself this: How many hours do you spend on cleaning and laundry a week? What if you could invest that time in your business, or set those hours aside for your family? What's that worth? Basic cleaning packages are available in most areas for about the cost of getting a dog groomed. If you're looking at this from purely a financial standpoint, see if the money you can make during each extra free hour exceeds the cost of housekeeping. If it does, it's a wise move.

Check out a variety of services for cost comparison and ask around for referrals–you'll want someone you can trust in your home.

If it's not distraction, it's dat-traction

Imagine the perfect work-at-home couple: They wake up at 6 a.m., Monday through Friday, well-rested, bright-eyed and eager to start the day. While he takes the spaniels for a walk, she makes a hearty but low-fat breakfast. The kids, already showered and dressed, join Mom and Dad at the table to eat, and share in relaxed but engaging conversation about what everyone plans to do that day. After breakfast, he clears the plates and stacks the dishwasher, while she drives the kids to school and the spaniels head into the living room for a nap. She returns, they both wash and groom, then they exchange a lingering kiss and head to their side-by-side desks in their neat-as-*Home Beautiful* office and spend the next eight hours hard at work, with the only interruptions being lunch and an occasional, "I love you," breaking the silence.

Idyllic as it might sound, it's also impossible. That's because most homes are fair game for distractions unthinkable in your average corporate office–at least, unthinkable beyond the receptionist's desk. Who can it be now? Telephone solicitors offering everything from long-distance phone service to cemetery plots. Grade-school sports teams selling chocolates door to door. The next-door neighbor who drops by before she leaves for her job to ask you to take in her packages when the UPS truck gets here. Your sister, who just happens to be in the neighborhood that day.

A home office of two has a better support system than any single homeworker enjoys, but it doesn't come close to the wall of defenses most employees in downtown highrises take for granted. There is no security gate, unless you're

Slobs vs. Neat Freaks

Stephen King. No reception desk. No oversized appointment board to notify visitors that you're "In Conference." It's just the two of you, with nothing but your front door and voice mail to defend you from interruptions. And, sometimes, even your own partner can end up being a distraction.

Susan Detwiler learned all too quickly how hard it can be to avoid interruptions. Just one week after she moved into a new house and a first-time home office–joining her husband, Mark, who already ran a home-based mail-order business–she found herself contending not only with a new work routine, but also with her children's winter break. Then, workmen began traipsing through the house to take care of a myriad of repairs and improvements. And, just when it looked as if the children would go peacefully back to school, a bitter cold spell hit and classes were canceled for several more days. More than a month after she and her family had settled into the new house, she says, "I think I've had a total of five or six days at home without the kids."

Though they're not usually as demanding as children, pets also can pose a threat to home office peace and quiet. Every day, we have to race to slam our office doors shut when one of us is on the phone and our three dogs start barking at the mail carrier, the Dalmatian that dares to live in a house across the street, or the plastic bag that blows through the backyard on a windy day and attaches itself to a shrub. And the dogs' up-the-stairs, down-the-stairs, round-and-round-the-house chases could stack favorably next to any got-you-last fight among brothers and sisters.

At least we can lock the dogs out of our offices for a while when things get busy without having to worry about them climbing onto and falling from the cookie shelf, or experimenting with the contents of the bathroom cabinet. Then again, we've found torn-up house plants–and worse–on the carpet on more than a few occasions when the dogs have gotten huffy about being denied access to the offices.

Little things you do to each other also can cross the line from quality time into distraction. Even one of the good points about working together at home–being able to pop into each other's office and talk whenever you feel like it–can have a downside. Susan Fletcher, who writes novels for young adults, says those friendly visits from Jerry or their daughter can be a real concentration-breaker when she's fighting writer's block. Just because she's sitting idly at the word-processor or playing a card game doesn't mean she's not working. In fact, her, "I'm thinking," phase is the worst time to interrupt her.

"When I play solitaire, it looks like I'm not working and I'm available for talking," she says. "Sometimes, when you're working, nobody can see the work going on." Jerry now knows to ask, "Can you talk now?" when he finds Susan sitting quietly in her office. He also has hit upon another way to make sure no one interrupts her productive silence: a "Do Not Disturb" sign for her office door. When it's displayed, he knows not to bother his wife. "It works for our daughter, too," Susan says. "It's amazing, the authority of this sign." Another couple has installed a stoplight outside each of their office doors, and anyone who runs a red runs the risk of encountering the long arm of the law.

Sometimes, the distractions are ones neither partner complains about: a long stroll to the park on the first warm and sunny day of spring, a trip to see a new movie in the afternoon when seats are cheap, a romantic interlude. All of these are undoubtedly pluses of working together, the benefits of being partners and your own bosses. But if the long stroll happens on Monday, the romantic interludes every afternoon and the matinee on Friday, you could be spending too much time playing and not enough working. In the long run, that could hurt your business, the very vehicle that allows you such benefits in the first place.

Dings, rings and other distracting things

Sooner or later, most Home Team couples figure out how to balance work and play, and how to limit unwanted interruptions from others in the house. Dealing with distractions from the outside, though, can be difficult–especially because there are so many of them.

Calls from telemarketers and fund-raisers are among the most annoying interruptions. You're home all day, so you're a captive audience. And once one company has figured out there's a live person at the end of your number, the word magically spreads to dozens of others. While even the shyest of home entrepreneurs learns how to say, "Sorry, I'm not interested, bye," after the hundredth interruption or so, keeping social calls in check is tougher. You don't want to be rude to your friends or family.

Vicki and Steve Palmquist have found that, the longer they've worked for themselves, the more they have gravitated toward friends who also are self-employed. People who work for themselves just understand the lifestyle better, they say. "A number of our friends don't understand why you can't (always) take off in the middle of the day and go to lunch," Vicki says. Steve adds: "It's a different concept for them. We don't want them to think we're business dweebs, but maybe we're less frivolous. We're more conservative with our time."

Today on Oprah: unemployed daughters

If you think friends are difficult to convince of the need for self-discipline in a home office, try the concept on family.

"My mother seems to have the hardest time understanding that I'm working at home, but for the wrong reasons," Vicki Palmquist says. Her mother's impression, she says, is that Vicki can watch soap operas and talk shows throughout the day.

Even with tens of millions of people now working in home offices, that remains a hard-to-kill misconception: you're not really working if you're at home all day. Or your work is somehow less important than it is for anyone who holds a job.

Early in our business, a teacher asked Shirley's youngest sister what Big Sis did for a living. Upon hearing that Shirley was a writer who worked at home, the teacher's response was, "Oh, she's unemployed." There probably isn't a Home Team around that hasn't received a similar reaction at some point in their work-at-home careers.

Colleen Larson still hears those, "As long as you're not busy ... ," remarks, although she has learned to be more firm when she is plied with non-work-related demands on her time. "People think I can just drop what I'm doing and go wherever," she says. "You have to learn to say no."

Margaret Hanson, a former stay-at-home mom who has a full-time home business with her husband, says it's especially hard to get adult children to understand she is working. "People think, 'Oh, you just have a hobby,' which it isn't at all," she says. She has learned to be tough with such comments. If she's hard at work and facing a deadline, she has no qualms about telling whoever calls that she's busy and can't change her schedule.

That's not to say there aren't times when you can–and want to–rearrange your day to accommodate a visit from friends or an impromptu lunch out with Mom. That's part of the joy of working at home. Just make sure your family and friends know the ground rules first.

"We tell all our friends, 'Please call before you come,' " Carlos Frey says. His wife, Sherian, adds that most of them are pretty good about doing that now–which is fortunate, considering the Freys occasionally start work before getting fully dressed. "Sometimes, I'm still in my nightgown at 1 in the afternoon," Sherian says.

Given time, even the most skeptical of relatives might one day understand you don't have to wear a tailored suit and commute downtown to be working. In the Palmquists' case, it took about five-and-a-half years since the start of their word-processing business, but the family is starting to come around. "I think some of them are realizing we're serious," Steve says.

Don't let work keep you from working

One more distraction needs mentioning, and that's work itself. You can be securely cocooned in your office as that deadline approaches, a big "Do Not Disturb" sign on the door, and your spouse outside ready to fend off any interruption ... and still find you're not accomplishing much. The phone keeps ringing as other clients call with new assignments or requests. Or it's the head of the company you're doing that report for, checking in with yet another update or change. Or it's your accountant, pelting you with dozens of questions she says need answering now so she can complete your tax return.

It's times such as these when you need to become your own sentry, standing at the gates sternly prepared to tell all comers, "None shall pass." Because, ultimately, if you don't jealously defend your work time, no one else will.

Sure, your partner can stand watch during those most frantic of moments when you're scrambling to complete a project–if his or her work is in a lull. But, sooner or later, the other phone will ring, and the lull will be over. And you'll have to step back into the gatehouse and again take hold of those keys to your sanity.

It's vital that you're serious about those times when you're not to be disturbed. Especially with the telephone. Many people can be drill-sergeant-strict about locking the office door, barring visitors and keeping themselves at the desk, but they turn into ninety-eight-pound weaklings the second the phone rings. No, you don't have to pick up the phone every time someone calls (nor do you have to open the front door if someone rings or knocks, another toughie for most). Let your answering machine or voice mail handle the calls. And if you don't have either of those services, get one. No one can or should be available twenty-four hours a day, and every business today needs someone–or something–to handle the callers when you can't.

Make it a habit of becoming the caller rather than the callee. Or use e-mail to send and respond to messages at your convenience. If your business permits, let your answering machine act as your receptionist and call back whom you decide, at the time you decide and for however long you decide. This also effectively knocks telemarketers out of your life. If you must answer the phone during business hours, check into Caller ID, which is available through many phone companies. On a display, this service shows you the number, name, or both of the person calling. Telemarketers almost always block identification of their calls, so set a policy to ignore calls sent without names or numbers.

If you've never kept a log of how much time you spend on the phone, try it for a week or two. You'll be dumbfounded by the results. The telephone is both one of business' greatest tools and greatest time-wasters. Make it work for you by keeping it under control. Some home workers have had success setting aside a specific period near the end of each day to return calls.

Slobs vs. Neat Freaks

Drop-in business is another concern. It's hard enough for the small-business owner in a storefront to contend with those who want their time without appointments. When they drop by your home without warning, the challenges are multiplied. What if they catch you in the middle of changing the baby's diaper? What if you got a late start that morning and your hair is still wet and uncombed? What do you do?

Jo Lutnes, who started working at home as a business writer, remembers that people would show up at all hours with jobs for her. The traffic through her house finally grew too demanding, so she moved her business to an outside office. She continues to work at home with her husband at their other business, though, which has no walk-ins.

Other couples find that moving their offices home cuts down on unwanted foot traffic. Since relocating their photo studio into their Donnelly, Idaho, home, John and Gail Baker have discovered they don't get as many browsers just dropping by to check out the business. Such time-consuming interruptions occurred frequently before at their in-town studio. Now, John says, "we get the people who are really interested."

If your home business depends on walk-in traffic, make sure your customers understand when you're at home and when you're at work. For some, that means set hours for business visitors and calls. "We don't pick up the work phone after hours," Susan Detwiler says. "We don't pick up the home phone during the day. I feel that, if you're accessible at all hours, you've lost your privacy."

Private space is just as important as private time. Unless all of your clients or employees are immediate relatives or the closest of friends, they should be kept as much as possible in working areas–not living areas–of your house. Make your business presentations in your office, not your kitchen or family room. This will make life easier on the family, and

129

is more professional, to boot. And, if possible, have a separate exterior entrance for your office.

Organizer Thalia Poulos recalls one client who had a beautiful office addition built onto his house. Unfortunately, the only way into the office was through his bedroom. That wasn't a problem in the early days of business, but, as his company grew, he needed to hire an employee–who ended up traipsing through the bedroom every time a consultation with the boss was required. While an intercom system and e-mail solved the problem, Poulos offers the story as a warning: Think about what your business might become one day. Employees and walk-in traffic might not be a possibility now, but they could become a necessity five years down the road. If you want to stay in your home office when that happens, plan in advance. Make sure your space can be adapted to protect the privacy of your home.

Working out when you're working in

Just when you think you're really in gear–distractions under control, laundry and dishes washed and put away, your office a sanctuary of productivity–one more wrench might tumble into the works. While it might not seem important to the effective functioning of a happy, profitable Home Team, over time it can become a problem that hurts your self-esteem or, worse, your physical well-being.

The challenge: getting enough exercise and keeping healthy. It might sound like that old vitamin commercial ("My wife. I think I'll keep her."), but it's true–watching out for your health is vital ... and awfully hard to do when you're working at home.

Part of the reason, again, is that precious commodity: time. Just as most home-based entrepreneurs will choose the high-paying project over a bout with the laundry, they will also tend to keep working instead of working out, or taking

Slobs vs. Neat Freaks

time to prepare healthful meals if there are dollar signs or deadlines dangling in front of them. In the long run, that could mean thicker waistlines, flabbier arms and less stamina–unless your work involves starring in exercise videos.

When we first started working at home, we signed up with a local health club and had every intention of being conscientious and making the trek three or more times a week. Every trip ate valuable hours, though: a half-hour to the club, an hour there, a half-hour back, not to mention time to wind down, clean up and change. And on days when we had no other reason to go out, or Chicago's ever-so-nasty winter weather conspired against us, we skipped the trip and told ourselves we'd do it tomorrow, which we often didn't.

The health club a flop, we decided to try jogging. This was more convenient–a park with plenty of room was only a block-and-a-half away, but the weather interfered again–cold, rain, heat and more.

The next alternative was the worst of all: forget about exercising. We felt guilty, lethargic and flabby. So we searched for another way. We've settled on a cross-country ski machine in our family room. We can use it while we're reading, watching TV or talking to each other, and we've been working out consistently for years. We feel much better since we've started. That keeps us on track, and we escape to the outdoors on nice days either in place of or in addition to our normal workout routine.

Other Home Teams are happy doing something else. Sherian and Carlos Frey use their basement treadmill almost daily. Toby Myles goes out to aerobics classes. Others might prefer jogging or bicycling, or swimming in the backyard pool. It's just important to begin and stick to a workout routine after checking with your doctor. While it is a time investment, you will feel better and be more productive. And if you don't make the time to work out now, you're risking something worse than flab and lethargy: you're upping the chances of paying the ultimate price at a young age.

Many couples who work at home also start hearing strange voices coming from the refrigerator and pantry: "Scott, Scott, it's the Oreos. Rescue us." The urge always is there to munch when you're at home, and many Home Team couples find a few months into their enterprise that their bathroom scales must be broken. Ignore the voices: watch those eating habits.

Keep working toward solutions

The best way to deal with the potential work-at-home challenges we've discussed is to anticipate them, then map out a plan for attacking them before they arise. It might not be the perfect plan, but that's OK–you can revise as you go. What's important is that you talk together about the obstacles you can expect, and hammer out the solutions that will work best for you.

There is no one right way to organize your office, divvy up housework, stave off distractions and keep healthy and fit. Just as with most successful exercise programs or time management plans, the key is personalizing the solution. That's the only way you'll be likely to stick with it for the long haul, through smooth or rough times.

So what if, with every other couple you know, she does the cooking and he mows the lawn? If both of you prefer to reverse those roles, and the arrangement works for you, do it. So what if your teen-agers get a little bent out of shape the first time you lock your office door so you can meet a project deadline without being disturbed? Unless it's an emergency, they will adapt to your routine and–hopefully–come to realize you're doing this because you want to make a better life for your family. After all, you're home when your family

Slobs vs. Neat Freaks

really needs you, and you're in the best partnership possible—a love and work partnership with your spouse.

Just realize it's inevitable that, when both of you first set the boundaries and rules, some feathers might be ruffled. Friends who don't understand your need for routine might be upset the first time you say no to a lunch date. Relatives who think you spend your days sleeping in and watching TV may lay on the guilt if you don't run errands for family members who "really work." If you stick to your guns, they will eventually respect you for your hard work, determination and success.

That's especially true for kids. Seeing parents in a healthy, happy and thriving Home Team teaches children a lot about life, love and work. Such rewards are worth the considerable challenges of working at home with kids—which we take a closer look at in the next chapter.

THE HOME TEAM

Home Team Quiz 5: "Know How to Say 'No'?"

1) You're juggling three big projects at work and are feeling stressed. Your boss asks you to take on one more "because you're the best for the job." Do you ...
   a) Say a reluctant "OK," plan to stay at work until ten every night and call your spouse to cancel that weekend trip.
   b) Say an enthusiastic "OK" because you're the only one who can do the work right.
   c) Hem and haw before saying "OK"... then panic later because there's no way to handle the work.
   d) Say you appreciate the compliment, but you're wrapping up several other projects–could it wait, or could you recommend someone else?

2) Where do you keep important papers?
   a) They pile up on a stand in the front hallway.
   b) I first make photocopies for my safe deposit box, then lock the originals in my closet and keep the combination in a locket around my neck.
   c) I have some in the kitchen, some in the den, some in the attic, some in the basement ... I think.
   d) We keep all our papers in a big dresser in our bedroom so we can both find what we need.

3) What do you do when your child interrupts your telephone conversation because he wants a ride to his friend's house ... *now*?
   a) Cut short the call and drive my kid over.
   b) Clamp my hand over his mouth until I'm done talking, then lecture him for ten minutes on not interrupting and ground him for a week.

Slobs vs. Neat Freaks

c) Try to figure out with hand-signals and notes what he wants while I carry on my conversation.
d) Excuse myself briefly to remind him not to interrupt. Then, after I finish on the phone, talk with him about what he needs.

4) How do you respond when family members call your business a "wild pipe dream"?
 a) I find myself agreeing and doubting myself.
 b) It makes me crazy–I usually blow up and give them a piece of my mind for interfering.
 c) I try to explain what I'm doing ... but I'm not sure myself half the time.
 d) I change the subject and tell myself my future success will speak for itself.

Score:
Was **a)** on target? Hey, will you lend us a thousand bucks and wash our car? You seem to have trouble saying "No," and that could hurt your Home Team. Start practicing now, "N ... O," "N ... O," ... "NO!"

Did you choose mostly **b)**? Loosen up a little! It's great to know what you want and can do, but Home Teams need to be flexible and understanding, too.

Was **c)** your choice? Home Teams need goals and direction, which you need to work on. Decide what you do and don't want out of life. Then learn to speak up for yourself.

Did you answer **d)**? You've got the right attitude for a Home Team–control without inflexibility, conscientiousness without workaholism.

Chapter 6

Mom and Dad Day Care Inc.
How to Stay Productive While Enjoying the Wonders of Work-at-Home Parenting

When Keith and Jo Lutnes started working from their Columbus, Nebraska, home, they discovered the special joys–and challenges–of sharing an office environment with children. "Summer vacation was the roughest," Jo recalls. "But I had the most beautiful garden in town."

Her healthy, weed-free yard was a product of necessity: the need to give her kids something to do as well as teach them the importance of not interrupting Mom and Dad at times during work hours. Kids being kids, the Lutnes' three daughters–Shondel, Jessie and Ann–had a tendency to forget their lunches, tennis shoes or musical instruments, and would call from school to ask Mom to deliver the goods. During the summer, the interruptions grew more frequent.

Jo's solution was to introduce the kids to the family garden. She took her daughters outside and asked them to identify which plants were carrots and which were weeds. Mom gave a single instruction: pull out everything that wasn't a carrot.

Kids: part of your life, part of your work

Home Team couples we interviewed were quick to emphasize two points about work-at-home parenting: it is one of the most wonderful parts of the lifestyle, and it is a big-time challenge. It takes planning and creativity to juggle parenting and running a home-based business, but many Home Teams are up to the task. That's because moms and dads have found the payoffs far outweigh the costs: they're around when their kids come home from school, skin a knee or need to show off that just-a-little-lopsided, Popsicle-stick birdhouse they just made.

"Our kids never had to ask what we do for a living," says Eric Flaxenburg, who with his wife, Jean, raised five children while running the French Creek Sheep and Wool Co. in rural Pennsylvania. "It's almost as if we were farmers. ... The kids were, in a sense, part of it. They still are."

That's the plus work-at-home couples point to again and again: work and family aren't unnaturally squeezed into separate compartments. Even in the fast-changing corporate world, plenty of companies expect their employees to pretend as if spouses, kids and household matters disappear in a little puff of smoke as soon as business hours start—or whenever business calls. Those who take off a couple of hours here and there to care for a sick first-grader or spend a morning waiting for a plumber can find themselves looking less promotable and more expendable. Home Teams, on the other hand, have discovered a more meaningful way to work, one in which all elements of life are blended into a sometimes-crazy but far more satisfying routine.

"Being a mom-and-pop operation, we're able to weave our children into our lives, which supports the system and issues of everyday life," urban planner Ronald Lee Fleming says. "Our children are very involved in our work. That's one of the strong aspects of this." For example, the kids–Reynolds, Siena and Severine–might prepare lunch or spend time talking with a work visitor. Or maybe they will help pack Dad's bags for his occasional trips abroad. Sometimes, they even travel with him.

"It's a catechism in their development," Fleming says. "We use our environment as a teaching mechanism for them–it's a notion that the children are not an isolated phenomenon but part of the whole scheme of things.

"That has a basis in pioneer families," he continues. "One of the problems with middle-class kids growing up is alienation from their parents." Children who share space with their parents' work every day–who see first-hand what their parents do and get a chance to be a part of it–don't suffer from that sort of separation. For Home Teams who do it properly, the payoff means stronger family ties and a deeper appreciation among both adults and children of how the family pieces fit together.

"It feels very normal to us," says Julie Dorfman, who with her husband, Jerry Herst, operates a window covering business out of their Evanston, Illinois, home. Their two daughters have reached a point where they are old enough to help with mailings. While they don't work for Mom and Dad often yet, the experience and daily exposure to their parents' work give the girls a deeper insight into what it takes to support a family. "Our kids understand Mommy and Daddy have to work to pay for things," Dorfman says.

Encouraging kids to play a part in the family business doesn't mean giving them free rein in the home office, though. Otherwise, you'll never be assured of the time you need to make calls, prepare reports, research or simply think.

Children provide an inescapable grounding in reality for any Home Team that might tend to become consumed by work. Few things are better for getting you out of the office by 5 p.m. than a loud crash from the kitchen or that suspicious silence from the family room, where your kids were just minutes ago screeching and blasting the television. Even without the minor disasters, couples with kids find they're less likely to work much beyond school hours or the babysitter's quitting time.

Susan Detwiler says her fears of not getting to work on time or working too long dissolved quickly after she moved into her home office, joining her husband, Mark. Their children, John and Ann, proved good at ensuring she is out of the office by a certain time. "I've taught them when they want me to come home, that's the phrase they use: 'Mom, can you come home now?' " she says.

Susan Fletcher's schedule, while more flexible than when her daughter, Kelly, was a preschooler, still fits mostly within the constraints of school hours. "Usually, once Kelly gets home, the productive part of my day is shot," she says.

Whatever the challenges for Home Team parents, there is also a wonderful peace of mind that comes from knowing you're only seconds or minutes away from your kids when trouble strikes at home or school. Photojournalist Bob Sherman remembers how appreciative he and his wife, Carolyn, were to be at home while their son, Roby, was young.

"It's been a tremendous pleasure to know, as he was growing up, he wasn't a latchkey kid," Bob says. "There was always somebody here. If the school called and said he was sick, five minutes later we'd be at the school."

Jewelry designer Valerie Saint-Gaudens and her husband, Kenne Swink, have found the same rewards with their two daughters.

"We have been home with them from their birth, and feel incredibly lucky to have watched them grow up," Saint-Gaudens says. A housekeeper helps watch the girls during working hours, but Mom and Dad usually are available at a moment's notice. "I like being here to kiss owies and make lunch, and let them come on grocery trips," she says.

Who's watching the kids?

Home-based entrepreneurs generate justifiable envy among the corporate crowd, especially working parents. But their take on the lifestyle often is incorrect: "Oh, you're so lucky," the comments go. "You get to stay home with your kids while you're working. It must be so nice to spend time with your kids and not to worry about day care or baby-sitters."

Any parent who has tried to put in a quality eight-hour workday at home while watching a child knows better. You bet you're lucky. You *do* have the best of both worlds. But it doesn't mean you don't have to think about child care. Children are demanding, and they need someone to watch out for them.

The ideal way to combine work and parenting responsibilities will depend in part upon your children's ages and your individual situation. Babies and toddlers tend to be more demanding on your time and energy than older kids, but even teens need to be assured a share of your time and attention.

Everyone gets touchy when the subject of parenting comes up. The aim of this chapter is to spell out the options and challenges, and for you to decide what is best. We do hope, however, that you will avoid the extremes. At one end is the Home Team couple that overlooks the potential benefits and treats child care as if they were traditional working parents. At the other end is the work-at-home couple that enters the arrangement thinking they can do it all. Chances are good couples at both extremes are going to end up frustrated and missing out on plenty.

The greatest concern usually is supervision. If your children are young, is it best to find some way to juggle Mom's and Dad's hours so both can work full time *and* provide care? Should one of you cut back on duties to take over most of the parenting responsibilities? Can siblings be trusted to

Mom and Dad Day Care

watch one another? How does outside day care compare to an in-home baby-sitter or nanny?

If you want to be equal partners in your home business and can afford in-home day care, that might be the way to go. On the other hand, if you have been a stay-at-home parent and your spouse is simply moving an established business home, you might choose to continue focusing your energies on your kids while spending a few hours here and there helping out with the business. Or maybe you will settle on some solution in between, with both of you trading off work and parenting duties as necessary.

Some work-at-home couples settle on the traditional division of labor: Dad spends his day concentrating on business matters while Mom takes primary responsibility for the kids. That doesn't mean Dad doesn't fix lunch for the children, help them get dressed in the morning or pick them up from school–he may well do all that and more. But it's Mom who tends to drop everything and leave the office when the baby wakes up, or who closes shop for the day once the kids come home from school.

This approach has both benefits and drawbacks. The biggest plus is that Mom is there at a moment's notice to take care of any child-related matters, large or small, and gets the satisfaction of being with her children as much as possible. The biggest minus: it's overwhelming. Work-at-home moms who try to do it all find they suffer the same frazzled nerves of that 1980s corporate icon–the Supermom.

Women can reduce the stress by cutting back on business duties. That turns the work side of the Home Team into much less of a partnership, but it's often a temporary situation for couples. Once the kids are old enough to go to school for a whole day, Mom is back in business full time, or at least close to it.

But not all women find it satisfying to juggle business responsibilities with diaper-changing, lunch-making and

141

school-time chauffeuring. They love their kids but also need and want the stimulation of a career. In other cases, a home-based business might need the full-time efforts of both husband and wife to operate successfully–maybe because the business is just getting started and there isn't enough money to hire help. Whatever the reason, couples find other ways to solve the child care/work dilemma:

Out-of-home care

• **Outside day-care and preschool programs.** These work best as stop-gap measures, not full-time solutions. After all, there's not much benefit to the lifestyle when Mom and Dad work at home all day but the toddlers are shipped out of the house from 8:30 a.m. until 4 p.m. But when it's a couple of hours a day, or a few half-days a week, it can be wonderful for freeing up some much-needed quiet work time. While these programs can be expensive, it's also comforting to know the service is there when you need it. Finding consistent day-care help can be difficult.

Make sure you check out many facilities before picking one, and make certain the business is licensed. Talk in depth to the people who run the programs to feel them out and determine whether you trust them with your kids.

• **Day-care home businesses.** Some with a love for child care and the entrepreneurial spirit combine these into a business venture. This option gives your kids the chance to spend their days in a home-like setting. And, of course, you would be supporting a fellow home business operation. Talk to the business owner, and ask for referrals. As with the previous option, there will be kids of a similar age to yours for them to play with, which can be fun. On the downside, expect your kids to get sick more frequently from the germs they will bring home from out-of-house day care.

- **Baby-sitting co-ops.** While not a business, the concept is similar to home day care. A group of parents in a subdivision or given area band together to form an organization in which they take turns watching the kids in homes. You save money this way, but you have to commit to doing your baby-sitting share for the crew every so often. On the downside, your kids have someone different watching them all the time, and you can't be certain how qualified the adult baby-sitters are. You might be able to start your own co-op by finding other work-at-home parents, or church members who live in your area and have kids of a similar age. If you have a homeowner's association, contact your board of directors or check the association newsletter to find out if anyone has started a co-op.
- **Friends/neighbors/relatives.** These will give you the greatest peace of mind of all the out-of-home choices, as you know your kids are either nearby, or with a friend or loved one. You can either pay someone or swing a child-care trade. Certain relatives, such as Gram and Gramps, might be more than happy to watch the grandkids for free.
- **After-school care.** For school-aged children, there are a myriad of after-school programs available. Check with your kids' schools, or local park district. No matter what grade levels your kids are in, there are plenty of sports and club activities that can teach them and let them have fun while you wrap up work for the day.

In-home care

In the next chapter, we'll talk about ways to escape from the home office. While the home can be the perfect place to live and work, we all need to get out of the house sometimes. That also holds true for your kids, and the out-of-home care options we previously discussed not only will give you a much-needed break, but also add some variety to your children's lives.

We do hope, however, that out-of-home care is the exception rather than the norm–especially for children in the first five years of life. These are special days for you as a parent, and important developmental times for your children. Working at home gives you options two-career job couples do not have–primarily, to spend the day under the same roof. Let's look at some in-home options:

• **Juggle work schedules.** Home Teams who follow this approach work different shifts and take turns watching the kids. Maybe Dad will start at 6 a.m. while Mom makes breakfast, shuttles the older children to school and spends the morning with Baby. When 2:30 p.m. rolls around, Dad takes over child-care duty, transports the kids on the rounds of softball, soccer and ballet practices, then pulls something out of the freezer to heat up for dinner. Mom takes a break for the evening meal, then hits the office for a couple more hours before everyone settles down for the night.

Another variation on this solution is for Mom to work two long days while Dad assumes responsibility for the kids, then trade places for the next two workdays. On the fifth day, help might come in so both parents can share a full day in the office. Both Mom and Dad can get in a full work week, spend time with their kids, and invest limited dollars in child care. This plan can work well for couples with good time management skills. It will, however, restrict time you can spend with your spouse.

• **Adult help.** This can be an even better solution: it allows parents to work when they want and spend time with their kids when they choose, and know that another adult is in the house to lend a hand with child care. This also allows Home Team spouses to spend more time together.

Your kids are home with you, though not always in the office, and you know that someone qualified is taking care of

Mom and Dad Day Care

them. If you feel like slipping downstairs to share lunch with them, or are needed to soothe a bumped forehead, you are there in seconds. But when work deadlines strike, you can throw all of your concentration into doing what you have to do without worrying about when the kids will start fighting again, or what to make for an after-school snack. Cost and dependability come into play with this choice, however. Here are some options:

Nannies. Is it just us, or can this word no longer be said without hearing Fran Drescher's voice rattle through your head? Anyway, a nanny is a pricey but wonderful choice. You can go through an agency, which will do the screening but will add to costs, or you can take out an ad and do the interviews yourself. Either way, this service isn't likely to be cheap, but, if you can afford it, it can make life a lot easier–especially if you can find someone willing and able to help with child care *and* clean the house. Many work-at-home couples go to bed nights dreaming of a "Hazel" or "Alice" to appear in their lives.

Au pairs. A French term meaning, "cheap labor." Not really, but there is quite a debate about use of this service. Working through an agency, you agree to let someone from overseas live in your home at no charge, and you pay her a small salary for a set period of time, usually one year. In return, the person must help with household duties for an agreed-upon number of hours each week. Although there are rules intended to protect both sides, there have been plenty of reports of abuses–some workers claim the arrangement is just short of legalized slavery, while some homeowners contend they are not getting their money's worth. On the plus side, it can be a cost-effective way of providing consistent child care. But remember that you have to share your home with a stranger. If it works, it can be a wonderful experience for the au pair and your family. If not ...

Friends/neighbors/relatives. As is the case when your kids are sent to homes of a friend or family member, having one of these people watch your kids in your house can be comforting and a blessing. The trouble is, can you find someone who can help consistently? And if you have to pay, is it affordable?

• **Teenage help.** Teens and college-age students (and even mature pre-teens) can provide inexpensive help after school and during summers. The challenge is finding ones mature enough to handle the duties, and reliable enough to show up for work. Start a teen baby-sitting list–and make it a long one to give you options. Ask for referrals from other parents. (Although they might not want to risk losing their good sitters, and who can blame them?) Ask at church. Ask your neighbors. Call nearby high schools. Some homeowner's associations also maintain a baby-sitting list.

A good, long list will eliminate frustration when you can't find someone you like, as well as be a lifesaver for those last-minute personal and business needs. If you find good baby-sitters, compliment them profusely and don't be frugal. A few extra bucks here and there might make the difference between them picking your house or someone else's the next time they are in demand by both.

• **Siblings.** Older children can and should provide helpful child-care support, but take care not to overdo it. Many kids who were forced by rough circumstances to become little moms or dads to their younger siblings grew up resentful, or regretting lost chances at youthful fun. Let older kids know you expect their help once in a while. And, if they do a good job, remember to reward that come allowance time.

Setting guidelines

When kids are home during work hours, it is important to explain clearly what behaviors you determine to be acceptable. Let your kids know there's a tradeoff involved in having Mom and Dad home more–a set of guidelines the kids must follow.

For Home Teams, when there are no such rules, there tends to be trouble. It isn't fair to the kids, because they have not been told what is expected of them, and it isn't fair to the parents, because they have not allowed themselves an atmosphere conducive to getting their work done.

Here are some areas where Home Teams have found it beneficial to set guidelines:

• **Noise.** Kids should be able to play reasonably without having to whisper or walk on tiptoes until 5 p.m. On the other hand, blasting the stereo, playing video games at top volume, shrieking, and loudly racing up and down the stairs should be out until the workday is over (if not entirely). If you're fortunate enough to have a large house or expansive yard where kids can be boisterous without the noise carrying into your office, great. But, otherwise, you need to set clear rules on how loud play can be. Too much noise ruins your concentration, creates a poor impression for clients who overhear the din and gives your home office a less-than-professional atmosphere.

When one of their sons was learning the drums, Michelle and Jim Foy established rules about when he couldn't play. Ordinary fun and games among their three children also could create distractions at times. "The biggest disadvantage is that, every once in a while, they'd get into a roughhouse," Michelle recalls. For the most part, though, "the kids have always been considerate."

Here again, it helps to have a clearly defined workspace that allows you to keep some distance from activities in other parts of the house. Susan and Mark Detwiler discovered those advantages after moving into a larger house where their offices were well-separated from the family room and recreation room where their two kids play. They've found it easier to keep working during that hour-and-a-half between the moment their children come home from school and quitting time.

• **Interruptions.** When you're in the middle of a big project and can't be disturbed, your children should know it. Most families want and expect the occasional walk-in from kids who have just come home from school, have to ask an important question or need help settling a fight. But you should make it clear when interruptions are not allowed.

Some Home Teams rely on a closed door to send that message, while others prefer a "Do Not Disturb" sign or even a locked office. Kids must know what the, "I can't be interrupted" signal means, and be taught to respect it at all times, except for a true emergency. As information broker Susan Detwiler says, "If the door is closed, I'm not to be disturbed unless they're bleeding."

While children can learn valuable life lessons from seeing their parents working together every day, the flip side is that they might take Mom and Dad's work duties for granted. It's a side-effect many Home Teams have noticed: the kid who barges into the office oblivious to everything but the fact that he wants to go to a friend's house *now* and needs someone to drive, or the child who drops casual comments about how her parents aren't *really* busy. Hey, if some parents, friends and neighbors can't figure out what we do, can we expect more from kids?

"They couldn't tell the difference if we were in the studio or at home," says Sherian Frey of her two boys, who were three and six when she and her husband, Carlos, opened an art studio in town. That attitude grew when the Freys moved their business home and still reveals itself now that their children are in their twenties.

One day, a representative from a major greeting card company visited the house to discuss possible marketing plans for the Freys' figures. During the meeting, one of the Freys' sons casually walked in and began talking to his mother. "He just thinks I'm at home," Sherian says.

Mark Detwiler recalls similar experiences with his two children the first summer they did not attend camp while he ran his mail-order business from home.

"It was tough–they didn't understand it was my job," he says. When they got bored, they would turn to Dad for entertainment, asking if he could drive them to the video store or baseball card shop. "It seemed like they didn't want to accept the fact that, 'No, I'm working.' "

• **Office visits.** When you allow your kids to drop in while you're working, it's important to set guidelines about their behavior in your office. Depending on your kids' ages, you might want to prohibit them from using or even touching certain pieces of office equipment, especially computers, printers, scanners, copiers and the like. At some point, this equipment will become fine teaching tools, but they are not for the young to toy with, nor for unsupervised use.

It also helps to have some rules about what kids may do while visiting and how long they may stay. A fifteen-minute stay while working quietly on a puzzle might be enjoyable to most parents, but an hour spent playing squawking video games and asking interminable questions should be out. Time together between parent and child during work hours should be special, not confrontational.

• **Telephones.** It is imperative to have separate telephone lines for home office and personal use. Kids should never answer a business line, nor should their voices be heard on the outgoing voice mail or answering machine message. For families who have only one line, children should be taught to stay away from the phone while you're working. Few things irritate business clients like the sound of a mumbly four-year-old answering the phone or picking up an extension. And asking a teen-ager to get off the line because you're expecting an important business call is a guarantee for civil war in your home. Kids also should know not to interrupt while you're on the telephone unless it's an emergency.

- **Activity schedules.** Kids today rarely seem to while away the hours building forts or playing ball in the backyard, or hanging out at friends' houses: they don't have the time. Just as their parents do, modern children have schedules to follow–play dates to keep, music lessons to take, soccer teams to practice for. Whether too much of this is good for kids is an argument we won't take on here, but it can certainly be a drain on work-at-home parents.

One way of controlling these time demands is to establish the "no surprises" rule. In other words, if a child doesn't let you know in advance that she's got a play dress rehearsal she absolutely has to go to on Thursday afternoon, she can't expect you to drive her there. Try to plan for such activities at least once a week by sitting down with your kids to discuss what school, sports and social appointments are coming up. While it's OK to make an exception from time to time, getting into the habit of breaking the no-surprises rule during work hours can quickly become disruptive and costly to business.

Guidelines will be much easier for kids to accept and for you to enforce if kids understand why the rules are there in the first place. Avoid the "because I said so" syndrome here. Always emphasize to your kids that they are an important part of the Home Team. Tell them that, when they let you work when you need to, they will be rewarded with more one-on-one play time, or favors during breaks and at the end of the workday.

Remember, whatever child-care solutions you settle on, that you chose to be a Home Team because you wanted a better life and a better lifestyle ... for everyone in your household. If your child-care choice is not working for you or someone else in your family, find out why, and look to either modify or change the approach. Network with other work-at-home parents. Go online and exchange tips with parents in forums dedicated to home-based businesses. Take a step back and size up your situation as objectively as you can.

And don't try to be perfect. If your kids are loved, well-looked after and business is going great, don't beat yourself up about the dust on the stereo, the day-old dishes in the sink or the fact that you've eaten carry-out for dinner three times this week. Running a business isn't easy. Neither is parenting. If you're doing both, your marriage is solid and everyone is reasonably happy, you're a great success.

Now that we've talked at length about keeping you at home more often, let's look at some ways to get you out of there ...

The Home Team

Home Team Quiz 6: "What About the Kids?"

1) How do you handle your kids at social gatherings?
    a) I don't–children should be seen, not heard.
    b) We include them in everything–weddings, dinner parties, evenings out with friends.
    c) We make sure it's fun for them–if there are no games, cartoons or children's menu, we won't go.
    d) We do a lot of fun things with them, but they also know some events are just for adults. They'd rather be home playing or making popcorn with the baby-sitter or their grandparents, anyway.

2) Have your children ever visited your workplace?
    a) No, I can't be bothered with that.
    b) My kids hang out in my office every day after school–they like to play games on my secretary's computer or chase around the warehouse.
    c) No way–they're bored to tears if there's no TV to watch or no other kids to play with.
    d) I've taken them to the office on special days–like Take Your Daughter to Work Day–and given occasional tours to show them what I do.

3) How do you handle disputes over what to watch on TV, or who gets to use the telephone?
    a) What disputes? We watch what I want, and my kids hang up the phone the second I tell them to.
    b) The kids have the TV until they go to bed, then I can watch. I sometimes use the car phone if my kids are tied up in a conversation for a long time.
    c) Oh, we don't have disputes. All our kids have their own TVs and telephones in their bedrooms.

Mom and Dad Day Care

d) We try to find shows we all enjoy together, but our kids spend more time reading and playing. We keep phone calls to a half-hour, and the kids understand they might have to hang up if something important comes up.

4) How could your kids help in your business?
   a) They'll do whatever I tell them–I'm the boss.
   b) I'll leave it up to them. If they want to answer the phone, play on the computer or mess around with the fax machine, that's OK.
   c) Oh, I wouldn't expect them to do any work–they'd just whine and complain anyway.
   d) I'll encourage them to try their hand at age-appropriate tasks. When work requires my full attention, though, I'll make sure they have constructive things to do elsewhere.

Score:
Did you say **a)**? Take it easy. Kids aren't miniature adults looking for full-time jobs with your Home Team. Let this lifestyle be fun for them, too.

Was **b)** the best match? A successful home office can't let kids have free rein–you might want to prepare them for home office realities.

Did you select mostly **c)**? Will you buy your kids little computers and company cars so they won't want yours? You can't provide constant entertainment *and* run an efficient business at home.

Was **d)** your answer? You've struck a good balance–you treat your kids with respect, but realize they're still just kids and need fair and loving guidelines. Your Home Team will be a great teaching tool.

Chapter 7

Getting Away From It All When It's All at Home

Michelle and Jim Foy don't often jet to Tahiti when they need a break from their consulting business, but they do make a point of getting away from their work regularly–even if it's only for an afternoon.

"A vacation to us, we don't need to go away to the islands and leave it all behind," Jim says. Instead, they take frequent little breaks to keep their lives balanced. "We don't want to let the pressures build up," he adds.

That could mean closing shop early one afternoon to go out and see a movie when admission is cheap, singing in their church choir or renting a stack of videotapes. "Both of us are vidiots," Michelle says. "We love Blockbuster. We tend to get tons of movies. They're like mini-vacations."

As with the Foys, photojournalist Bob Sherman appreciates the importance of not overworking: "We're not slaves to our businesses. We put in a lot of hours, but we take off when we want to."

They are better than most, though, at scheduling free time. Many work-at-home couples *know* they should give themselves a break every now and then, but somehow never

Getting Away From It All

get around to doing so. Those who don't work at home tend to wonder how Home Teams avoid slacking off, but more often, the opposite is true: many Home Teams don't know when to quit working. "We're one family in need of a sabbatical," Ronald Lee Fleming says. "It's hard to escape."

This is a problem that can evolve out of a Home Team benefit–some couples love what they do so much they can't bring themselves around to punching out for the evening or weekend, much less for a week's vacation. They enjoy their work, and they enjoy working together. So why should they ever stop the fun? But even a day in Disneyland can be exhausting–after eight or ten hours of popcorn, Pluto and the Pirates of the Caribbean, it's good to get back to the hotel and read, or lounge around the pool. Everybody needs a change of pace from time to time, for variety and to keep a healthy perspective on life.

"That's what bed-and-breakfasts are for," Colleen Larson says. She and her husband, Jerry, don't find it necessary–or practical–to escape their sculpting work for days on end. But they can take a breather during even their busiest seasons, as they did one Christmastime when they booked a room at a local inn. They stayed home and worked during the day, but they headed to their cozy getaway when evening came.

"It was great," says Colleen, adding that the change of scenery even gave them an opportunity to do a little free word-of-mouth advertising with other hotel guests when the subject of who did what for a living came up.

But a love for their work isn't the only obstacle to Home Teams who need a break. There's also a very practical reason some couples go almost non-stop, and that's because–unlike their 9-to-5 corporate counterparts–they don't get paid for not working. There are no sick days, no paid vacations, no sabbaticals. If they want to keep earning, they have to keep churning.

"It's a double whammy," Jerry Fletcher says. A vacation means not only time off from work–which can lead to an overload of catchup duties before and after leaving home–but also a week without pay.

That's something couples who work at home have to get used to, unless their business has the potential for residuals that keep the money flowing long after the work is done. But so what? You don't sign away the rights to leisure time when you start a home business. People who work at home can–and must–take vacations. It just requires a change in thinking.

It means saying, "OK, I realize I won't have a paycheck waiting for me when I get back from Montego Bay, but if I work smart that's no reason not to go." It also means realizing that, "I might have to hustle twice as hard the week before and the week after my vacation, but I'm not taking my work with me." A week in Jamaica with a laptop computer and a stack of paperwork is not going to make you feel as if you've left the home office, and it's not going to give you your money's worth of R & R for the investment you've made.

Still, if opportunities for escape are limited, work-related trips provide a much-needed break for some Home Teams. Artists Carol Kurtz and Steve Mudd say they would like to get away more, but can't manage a full-fledged holiday at this point in their business. "Anything like a significant vacation is right out of the question," Steve says. However, their work takes them to the Renaissance Fair in Minnesota for several weekends every summer to market their creations, and they look forward to the trips. Even Carol's teen-age son enjoys those weekends, which also reunite them with fellow artists who have become good friends through the years.

"The Renaissance Fair is sort of an addiction," Carol says. "I love it. The people are insane. We get to be with friends all weekend. It's a support group, also." Steve agrees: "If we won the lottery tonight and won eight billion dollars, I would still go to the Renaissance Fair."

As an added bonus, consider that work-related travel can offer plenty of tax deductions. As long as the trip has a legitimate business purpose, portions are deductible. Check with your tax adviser. This is a nice incentive for Home Teams to take a business trip every now and then.

Getting away doesn't have to mean packing a suitcase or making hotel reservations, though. "How do we get away? Movies, dinner dates with each other and taking walks give us time together," says craft supplier and artist Dan Carlson. "The workday usually ends when it ends. If we schedule ahead of time, we usually can end it when we want to."

Others find the refreshment they need by keeping their weekends work-free–admittedly, not an easy assignment, especially for the newborn work-at-home business. However they handle the balance of work and play, though, it's the couples who realize the importance of both who are happiest with all aspects of their lives.

The key is planning–for fun as well as work. Figure out when you want to get away, then do everything you can to make it happen. Avoid scheduling projects for the days you will be gone, and give yourself enough time to finish the work in advance. With longer vacations, if you have a trusted subcontractor or assistant, make sure he or she will be available and prepared to put out any unexpected fires that ignite in your absence.

If not, give your clients adequate notice that you will be unavailable for a short time ... but *don't* give them your hotel phone number. We made this mistake once during a week-long getaway to Florida, and–even though our clients never called–felt edgy the whole time we were gone. We pushed it to the back of our minds, but the thought was often there: when will they call and what will they want? It's sometimes hard enough for us to get away from work during the supposed "off hours" at home. Allowing work to follow us on our vacation left us feeling cheated.

Getting away takes effort. Even with planning, vacations from the home office are loaded with challenges the average bank teller or school principal never encounters, as Vicki and Steve Palmquist discovered. They hadn't taken a vacation from their writing and desktop publishing business in four years when they decided to get away for a week. Vicki prepared by sending letters to their clients notifying them of their plans–and almost ended up regretting it.

"It was as if they felt we were going to die when we went on that vacation," she recalls. Clients piled on the work in the weeks beforehand until the Palmquists almost went crazy. But the couple learned from their ordeal: they're experimenting with shorter, four-day getaways that aren't preceded by such mind-numbing stress.

The Palmquists' experience illustrates the biggest roadblock to work-at-home couples looking for a break: time off doesn't just happen. It might be easy at a job–with your boss' OK–to simply mark your week off on the company calendar and go, but taking a holiday from a home-based business requires more preparation.

Susan Fletcher acknowledges she and her husband, Jerry, haven't gone on vacation for some time "primarily for lack of planning." Even one day of leisure with their daughter, Kelly, requires scheduling. "I think we need to plan for fun things to do on the weekends," she says. Otherwise, it's all too easy for work to slip over into Saturday and Sunday.

It might not feel carefree or spontaneous to make an appointment for an afternoon at the beach or evening at a nice restaurant, but for couples who otherwise would never get away from work, it's a necessity. The two of you need to make a habit of looking through your calendars together and setting aside regular playtime, even if it's for only an hour or two.

Getting Away From It All

Whatever the hurdles, the Home Team lifestyle offers more flexibility than any other work arrangement when it comes to getting away from it all. It erases such corporate-style complications as established work hours and vacation restrictions. And while there will be limitations, work-at-home couples have eliminated a lot of the old middle men. If anyone decides whether it's a good idea to take off a week around Christmas, for example, it will be you two–not your supervisor at work who won't schedule the time because she's taking off that week, and she has seniority. Why wouldn't any Home Team want to make the most of a deal such as that?

"The biggest advantage of working at home together–freedom," jewelry designer Valerie Saint-Gaudens says. She and her husband, Kenne Swink, transfer their order-line calls to their cellular telephone when they want to leave the house for a while. They've also hired a jeweler, which gives them greater flexibility to take trips and mini-vacations as small as going down to the harbor for a long lunch.

Saint-Gaudens and her husband eat lunch out often. They also regularly schedule activities on their days off. "When you work at home, you have to leave on the weekends probably more than most people," she says. "So we get the family out of here almost every Sunday."

Getting away *from* work is only half the equation. What Home Teams are getting *to* plays an equally vital role. Are you still seeing good friends? Do you maintain relationships with others in your field, whether those associates are in home offices or high-rises? Are you keeping in touch with the outside world as much as you would like, or do you feel as if you're locked away in a golden tower–even though it's with the love of your life and the best business partner you could ever have?

Work-at-home couples have a lot going for them, but they will always need more than just each other, twenty-four hours a day, seven days a week. Face it: the arrangement wouldn't be very appealing to the average husband-and-wife team if it meant living like hermits, even minus the bug-and-berry diet, and cave accommodations.

"It's important to keep up with relationships," Michael Desgrosseilliers says. "Sometimes you get so wrapped up in what you're doing, you forget everyone around you." He adds that he and his wife, Marjorie, make a point of having outside interests and getting away occasionally. He watches and plays sports, and she's active in their church. They also sing together in the church choir.

Keeping in touch with the "real world" will mean different things to different people. Maybe you were never big into socializing even when you worked outside the home; for you, a phone conversation or two with a colleague every week and dinner out with friends every few months or so is enough. Or maybe you crave contact with people; you're happy with your home business as long as you know you've got bowling on Monday night, dinner with friends on Tuesday, yoga class on Wednesday and so on.

Of course, it's not unusual for the first type to be married to the second type–another reason Home Teams need to be flexible both in the office and outside of it. The two of you might love working side by side every day, but if your partner needs no more after-work diversion than a good book and a roaring fire, and you go bats without daily forays into the outside world, both of you will have to learn to set aside more time for yourselves.

Alex Censor says he and his wife, Meera, sometimes have different ideas about how to relax because their businesses are so different. As a reviewer of computer software, he spends more time in their San Diego home than does Meera, who gets out periodically for one of her pursuits: massage therapy. When he's ready to take a break, he wants to escape the house, while Meera might be more content to stay in. For the most part, though, they love the freedom their work-at-home arrangement offers and try to take advantage of it regularly–as a team. "I like the companionship and energy we share together," Meera says. "Alex is the man of my dreams. We do everything together."

A lot of couples say the same thing: even when they get away from work, they usually go as a team. But many also schedule individual downtime that allows them to stay in touch with separate friends or pursue personal interests.

"As I spend most of my time out with clients, meeting people is not a problem," says Robert Timothy Wickes, who with his wife, Nina Tinsley-Wickes, runs an information management consultancy from their home in England. "For Nina, her business is a lot on the phone, and therefore she needs time to meet people and get out. She does this by taking specific time off to go shopping or garden, or enjoy some other recreational activity." Robert has pursuits of his own, including association lunches and meetings.

James Patterson says he and his wife, Toby Myles, try to make sure they each have at least one full day to themselves every month. Each of them might go out with friends, or Toby might attend an aerobics class or work on her jewelry-making skills.

"It's important that you be able to do your own thing," Susan Schandel says. While her husband, Terry, spends his free time working on electronics projects, she likes to go to the ballet, group meetings or church.

Keeping in touch with others–whether together or individually–can be tricky for Home Teams. Working at home means you're automatically out of the typical office social loop. No more company picnics. No more bulletin board invites to happy hour at a local pub. And, depending upon the type of work you do, you might not have many opportunities to get out and meet people.

But there's more to it than that: Anyone who starts working at home undergoes mental changes along with the change in office address. You're in charge now, you've created your own office environment, and your work is always there. You become a different person in some ways, and you might find you can no longer relate to some friends and associates. You might find you and your former co-workers just don't have that much in common anymore, now that you can't share horror stories about that new busybody down the hall, or gripe about the company's latest move to cut costs by rationing pencils.

Ronald Lee Fleming agrees that finding social outlets got tougher when he moved to a home office: "You have to take more initiative to meet other people. When you have the family at home and work at home, you're more likely to get isolated."

On the other hand, Susan Detwiler says she has increased involvement with others in her line of work. In the corporate world of market research, she and her co-workers were discouraged from talking to colleagues at other companies. "I've found that I have more colleagues now that I'm on my own," she says. Most of her professional contacts are electronic–via telephone or online–but she's also active with an association and serves on its board of directors. Together, these contacts provide a satisfying social outlet.

It takes special effort as a Home Team, but you can expand your social horizons in many ways. Try joining professional associations, or local work-at-home or entrepreneurial organizations. It can be a real boost to meet other home-office types and swap stories about the benefits and challenges of work-at-home life. If you don't care for a lot of socializing, you can feel more plugged in by receiving newsletters that will help you professionally, or improve your lifestyle. Joining a network or industry group also can aid you–it's a good way to keep up with business trends and news when there are no more company memos or staff meetings to depend on.

Electronic contacts are another great way of staying plugged in, both literally and figuratively. With the Internet and a host of online computer services, there's a Web site, bulletin board, listserv or newsgroup for just about any type of profession or interest. And e-mail can connect you with associates all over the world, allowing you to do anything from send the occasional request for business tips once every few weeks, to chat nightly with electronic cohorts. Again, the way the world is changing, it's in your best interest anyway to stay on top of the communications revolution. What might be a diversion or social outlet today could become your top way of finding clients or distributing your products and services tomorrow.

If you're looking for social outlets that aren't work-related, there are just as many opportunities: churches, service organizations, book clubs, parents' associations, exercise groups, park district classes, sports teams and plenty more. Online, you're just a few clicks away from chat groups for everyone from pet owners and parents of twins, to sports enthusiasts and gourmet cooks. So it doesn't matter where you live or what you do–if you make a little time, there are plenty of ways to keep in touch with others.

Break time

No matter how much you love what you do, you and your Home Team partner need to get away at least a little from the responsibilities of your businesses and from the house itself. Depending on where you live, what you do and your financial situation, the type of break that's best for you will vary. It's the fact that you're taking one at all that's important. Just decide what kind of breathers are most effective, and plan accordingly:

- **The spontaneous break.** Work is slow and the weather is balmy, so you decide to take off early to lie in the sun in your backyard. Or a hundred-and-one little frustrations through the day have chipped away at your sanity, and you need to turn off the computer, switch on the voice mail and get out of the house. Do it. These little breathers don't have to take a lot of time–even an hour can work wonders when you're stressed–but they can act as a much-needed escape valve when home-office pressures become overwhelming.
- **The scheduled breather.** Again, these interludes don't have to eat big holes into your work time, but they will help you enjoy the special benefits of the work-at-home lifestyle. Plan to take a lunchtime break with your spouse to try out that new restaurant you have been hearing so many good things about. Or set aside time one afternoon to see the latest release at the movie theater–before the kids get out of school and way before the nighttime date crowd packs the house. Taken regularly, these little interruptions are an important way to preserve your mental health by getting you outside before your office begins feeling like a sweat shop.
- **The short getaway.** Wednesday's forecast is hot and sunny, while the weekend promises to be cool and soggy. So why not plan a mid-week day off to loll on the beach, and use Saturday as your regular workday instead? It's amazing how refreshed you can feel after one day in a different and work-free environment. And breaking up the week into two- or three-day segments also makes work go a lot easier.
- **The weekend.** For work-at-home couples, this can be the hardest break of all to take on a regular basis. Without occasional weekend breathers, though, it doesn't take long to feel as if you never can get away from your work or your house ... and to end up hating both of them. You might even

find yourself envying friends who work 7-to-7 corporate jobs Monday through Friday, and that's not a feeling you want to encourage if you plan on staying a Home Team for long. Do yourself a favor: set aside at least one weekend a month to play. You don't even have to go out–you can rent a stack of videotapes on Friday night and spend the next forty-eight hours in your pajamas, cozying up to each other on the couch. The important point is that you're not in your office.

• **The full-fledged vacation.** A magazine article for home entrepreneurs once described the vacation as a sign you were "making it." Really, though, it's more an indication of good long-term planning, which certainly is the kind of thing that leads to success. A vacation itself is no great accomplishment: there are plenty of teen-agers working full-time, semi-skilled jobs who can take a week off once they have put in enough time. Arranging your work schedule, preparing clients, budgeting extra money to escape your business for a while: those are the real signs you're "making it."

Again, a vacation doesn't have to mean the stereotypical week at the Grand Canyon or in Orlando. You might prefer spending the time sprucing up your garden during the day and experimenting with new recipes on the backyard grill every evening–doing anything at home but working. It's the computer, phone, calculator, fax machine or workbench you're getting away from.

Whatever type of respite you prefer, it's critical that you always schedule time for yourself. It's vital that–even on the most pressure-packed and crisis-filled days–you can look at your calendar and know there's a moment or two coming up that will allow you to escape. No work-at-home couple–or anyone, for that matter–should take pride in laboring non-stop for months or years without a break. Many of those ultra-workaholics from the '80s have figured that out–they have since scaled back their careers to raise kids and plant wildflower gardens. Besides, it's certainly not a selling point for the Home Team lifestyle when you tell office-working friends you're so busy all the time that you will never be able to meet them for dinner, go to that old co-worker's surprise party or join them for a quick game of tennis on Saturday. If you find yourself saying things such as that regularly, you need to focus on ways to add better balance to your life.

Another important point: breaks are not just for you, so the excuse that you don't feel the need to get away isn't a very good one. Think about your partner. Parents, consider your kids. If you're committed to the team part of the lifestyle, you have to be aware of the needs of everyone in your household. Make sure your work-at-home pursuits benefit everybody as no other career could. Otherwise, being part of a Home Team won't be any better than working two demanding, downtown office jobs that have been transported otherwise unchanged to your spare bedrooms.

Don't make Jack a dull boy

Do you ever find yourself saying, "There's no way I can ever get away"? You can sometimes find yourself facing a problem without an apparent solution because all the little things that could have helped you were neglected in the past. A home office can be filled with such traps ... unless you have prepared. When it comes to being able to take a break, make sure you have taken steps along the way that can set you free. Here are a few to consider:

- **Voice mail/answering machine/answering service.** Unless your business doesn't depend a bit on telephone calls, you're attempting the impossible by working without one of these. You will also need a willingness to ignore the telephone when you're taking a break; if you're in the middle of some much-needed free time, feeling the need to answer every call will frustrate you more than not having a breather to begin with. If your business depends on orders, it's a good idea to have a live voice on the line during business hours, so an answering service could be a must. Otherwise, don't fear voice mail. If the call is important, the caller will leave a message.

• **A planning calendar.** You don't have to rigidly pencil in work from 9 a.m. to 5 p.m. every weekday, with a half-hour for lunch and an hour for dinner (freedom from that type of constraining schedule should remain the beauty of working at home). But you should have a fairly clear idea of what you need to do every day and how long each job will take. That accomplished, you will have a better idea of where the best possibilities lie for free hours and days–and you can plan them. Then, you just need the resolve to stick to your schedule. Only real emergencies should interfere. Don't waste your days putting out every tiny fire someone else sets. You control your calendar.

• **A reasonably organized office.** No, you don't have to be the King or Queen of Neat. But if you can tell with not much more than a glance how much work has come in and how much needs to go out, you will have a better gauge of what your day and week will look like–and where you might have time for a break.

• **Delegation skills.** People who take pride in their work–especially if they are self-employed–tend to think they need to do it all. After all, it's their venture, their name on the business cards, their reputation. But it makes no sense for one Home Team member to struggle to finish three major projects if her partner-husband knows the business just as well, and just happens to be having a slow workday.

Realizing they can't do everything, smart home business owners also form ongoing and occasional partnerships with talented folks at other companies. You can contract with these people to handle tasks when you are overwhelmed or need to get away, or they can handle parts of the job you might not be as good at so you can focus your talents on other aspects of your business.

It's also needless wheel-spinning to spend valuable time licking envelopes, stapling reports or filing if there are old-enough children in the house who would be glad–especially with a little financial incentive–to help out.

• **Communication and coordination.** These are keys for any successful Home Team, in the office and out. The only way you will be taking breaks of any kind is if you and your partner stay in sync. You don't have to work identical hours, take lunch at the same time (though that's a nice perk) or both go to sleep the moment Letterman ends. But it's easier to enjoy time together if you warn your husband on Monday that, gee, Thursday looks like a slow day for you–any chance he might be able to schedule his week so you both can take off early for a picnic in the park?

If you have kids, communication and coordination are even more important–from all directions. You have the right to fair warning that a school musical or Little League game is set for a time you might normally be working, and they have the right to expect to share some time and fun with you. It helps to have regular family get-togethers to schedule events in everyone's calendar (kids should have these, too, and learn to use them). Sunday night is the perfect time for many to sit down and plan the week with the spouse and kids. Everyone's focus is past the weekend and on the week ahead.

• **An ability to say no.** Say it five times now–no, no, no, no, no. A simple two letters, but it certainly is one of the toughest words in the English language. If it were easy to say, you wouldn't have telemarketers calling you every thirty minutes, and you wouldn't have purchased that rust-proofing for your new car.

Don't make a habit of trying to be Superman, Superwoman or Supercouple. Yes, you need to work to pay the bills, but if you overload yourself with more projects than you can humanly handle, you will end up frazzled, sad, and–more than likely–unable to finish all your work satisfactorily. This will make your clients teary-eyed, too, before they go looking for someone else to handle the next job.

Be realistic about your work, even if it means turning down an occasional project or at least delaying the due date. Remember Jack Nicholson's example, even if you're not the caretakers of a mountain hotel: "All work and no play ... ."

Click those red shoes together and say, 'There's no place like ...'

Finally, just having a pleasant home makes it easier to get away from work on days you can't leave. You don't want simply a house–you want a home, a place where you can feel cozy and secure. If your house is starting to feel less homey and more like an office with a couple of extra rooms where you sleep and eat, you might want to consider some improvements.

"Because we are at home all the time, we have made our home really nice to be in," jewelry designer Valerie Saint-Gaudens says. "It's decorated well, and the yard is pretty. I have to have colors around that make me feel good."

Keeping your home a place you enjoy–even when you're working–should always be a priority for you and everyone in your family. That means more than just ergonomically designed desks, wrist-friendly computer keyboards and decent office lighting. Think about what's important to you, what you enjoy having around you. Maybe it's original art on your office walls. Perhaps it's an ever-changing woodland garden, or a gently bubbling fish pond right outside your office window. Maybe it's a comfy corner of the house where you can get together with your family and talk or play games. Think beyond just the big-screen television set as the focal point of the family room. What makes your home feel homey, even when it's also being used as an office?

Margaret Hanson says she and her husband, Bob, don't need vacations to escape the stresses of work. Their home in Shelley, Idaho, can be perfectly restful: "We live out in the country. It's kind of nice where we live, so we don't need to get away from people."

Another nice thing about gardens, family nooks and other little at-home getaway spots is that they can be works in progress, projects you can enjoy when your regular work is done. They help your home be a place to live, create and relax–as well as work–in.

In taking time to get away from work and savor life, remember to enjoy each other as more than just work partners. It can be easy to end up talking little else but shop and the kids, but most of us were together way before either business or children came around. Let's add a little spice ...

Getting Away From It All

Home Team Quiz 7: "Relax, Will You?"

1) Do you feel as if you never have time for fun?
   a) Fun? What's that? I work, I take care of the house and family, and that's that.
   b) We'd like to have more fun, but just can't afford to waste any time or money right now.
   c) Absolutely. We try to plan for fun family activities, but something always gets in the way.
   d) Sometimes. But we make a point of getting out at least once a week for something fun, and try to keep weekends free for family time.

2) What inspires you?
   a) Nothing. Success comes from sweat and sacrifice, not from a wave of some magic wand.
   b) Dreams of winning the lottery so I never have to work again.
   c) I wish I knew. I'm so busy putting out fires at work and home all the time, I never have a chance to stop and dream.
   d) I find inspiration everywhere. It could be a hug from my daughter, a story in the local paper, even a song on the radio I haven't heard since high school.

3) What's on your calendar for future fun?
   a) Ask me when I'm sixty-five and, hopefully, ready to retire.
   b) We're saving for a nice trip in ten years or so. Until then, though, it's work, work, work.
   c) Oh, I don't know. If things slow down in the next year or two, maybe we can get away to the

lake for a couple of days.
d) We've got at least one special weekend penciled in every month.

4) What would you change to have more fun?
a) Nothing. I can't fool around with work–there's too much to do and no one else to do it.
b) I was thinking about taking on a second job so we could afford a time-share in Florida.
c) I don't think I have any control over that. My responsibilities at work and home come first, and that rarely leaves time for anything else.
d) I work at it every day. I try to make sure I always have a break–even if it's only a half-hour walk–marked in my calendar each week.

Score:
Did you choose mostly **a)**? Lighten up, Francis! Remember, the Home Team lifestyle comes as a whole package: career and family and work and fun. Every part is vital to a healthy life.

Did you say **b)**? Back up. Money and unlimited free time don't guarantee fun. Happiness comes from balance in life, a balance of work, service and recreation.

Was **c)** a match for you? Make fun a higher priority in your life. Except for the rare emergency, last-minute requests for favors shouldn't constantly be hurting your own needs and your family's.

Was **d)** your choice? Give yourself a pat on the back for a realistic and balanced attitude toward life. Keep it up!

Chapter 8

Fooling Around at the Office
How to Ignite and Maintain Passion When You Work at Home

Romance seemed so easy when you were younger and dating, didn't it?

If you met in high school or college, you and your sweetheart could ditch class to enjoy afternoon rendezvous on warm spring days, eat lunch together every day in the cafeteria and hang out at all hours during summer vacation. If love struck you two in ensuing years, you probably did all you could to impress each other, and spent as much time together as possible. Love was all that really mattered.

Then ... adulthood, marriage, work, parenthood and the rest of the "real world" got in the way.

You ended up working long hours in separate places, maybe in different cities. There was the long commute back and forth–which ate up more valuable time. Not to mention overtime, business trips and the briefcase full of work you ended up slaving over at home at least a couple of times a week after dinner. Where did all the time go? All of a sudden, there were few opportunities for the shared lunch, the stolen afternoon of fun or the mid-day romantic interlude.

As we march further into adulthood and marriage—and especially when parenting enters the picture—most people tend to kick romance far down their priority list. Whereas at one point it was all they could think about, many somehow find romance scooted its way down the list to the neighborhood of washing the dog. Perhaps romance stays on hold until weekends, holidays and vacations roll around. Worse yet, maybe it vanished altogether.

In today's fast-paced world, it takes plenty of effort to keep romance alive, whether you work in a corporate setting or home office. Either way, romance can—and must—happen for you to keep happy and get the most out of marriage. Marriage counselors find over and over again that when romance disappears, other pieces of the marriage tend to tumble. When romance evaporates, spouses also are more likely to turn elsewhere for what they crave, and, too often, they find themselves in the arms of someone else who finds them sexy and exciting.

As yet another plus to the Home Team lifestyle, spouses who work together enjoy more and better opportunities for intimacy and romance than do their corporate counterparts.

That is ... if they commit to living a life of passion together and choose to take advantage of those chances.

Because Home Teams work together as well as live together, they share more than dinner, bedroom space and the occasional Saturday night family outing. They also can have common career goals and business-related experiences, as well as mutual home and family interests. They spend whole days and weeks, rather than a few evening hours and weekends, together. And they have their offices to themselves, if only for part of the day if they have school-aged-or-younger children.

All the ingredients are there for intimacy and romance. Whether Home Teams choose to be selfish, lazy, preoccupied and take each other for granted, or do all they can to inject excitement and spice into their lives is up to them. In this chapter, we wish to remind you to never forget or underestimate the importance of romance. We also will show you ways you can use your Home Team relationship to grow closer and keep your love life exciting.

Shared work, shared homes, shared lives

One of the benefits Home Teams point to again and again is that their unique work relationship has helped them learn more about each other than they ever expected. Yes, any couple that marries, raises children and grows old together gets to know each other pretty well. But sharing a full-time business and many hours a day with a person, day in and day out, creates opportunities for a deeper level of understanding than most 6 p.m.-to-6 a.m. couples can dream of. "We find that, the more time we have together, the better we get along," says James Patterson of his relationship with his wife, Toby Myles.

As with raising children, forming a Home Team is a learning experience. Not every step along the way is easy, but–done wisely–the result can be a richer, deeper, closer and more meaningful marriage. That's because the skills that make a good marriage are the same as those that create a successful Home Team: hard work, respect, patience, communication, and a willingness to listen and grow.

By sharing in both a business and a marriage, Home Teams can develop those skills around the clock. When you go to work together every day, there's no shelving away the critical remark made in the heat of an argument, or the nagging sense that something is bothering your spouse. You have a real incentive for facing both marriage and business conflict head-on, which might not always be pleasant or convenient, but in the end makes you both better spouses and business people if you handle issues properly and lovingly.

"We have no problem keeping romance alive," says Jeeni Criscenzo, who runs a graphic design and copywriting business with her partner, Joe. "Joe is a very passionate man who can easily turn me on. We never get tired of each other when it comes to that! It's the fire that makes everything else work. I know that sounds like bragging, but it's true. In fact, it seems that the respect we've gained for each other by working together has enhanced our physical relationship."

While any good marriage has to include mutual respect, the Home Team marriage can awaken both spouses to talents and gifts they never knew their partners had. A husband, for example, might know his wife has job-juggling savvy, but until he's working in a home office with her all day and sees her wash four loads of laundry, make dinner, balance the checkbook, change the twins' diapers and edit her company's annual report–apparently all at once–he might have a hard time appreciating just how talented she is. And a wife might realize that her husband's people skills have kept his business healthy, but until she hears first-hand how he soothes a foaming-at-the-mouth client over the telephone and rescues a shaky multi-year contract from the brink, she might not understand how amazing his abilities are.

Margaret Hanson says she was surprised by her husband's talents in clothing decoration after they started their embroidery and monogramming business. Bob, a retired naval officer, suddenly demonstrated great skill at creating designs for baby clothes and other items. "I didn't ever realize Bob would be as good as he is working with fabrics and colors," she says.

While seeing each other's talents is rewarding, Home Teams also can benefit from the up-close view of some of each other's shortcomings ... or what they perceive as such.

Nothing teaches patience for your spouse's approach to people, problems and life in general like sitting there watching when you're sure he or she is going to fail miserably ... but instead succeeds in ways you didn't think possible. Maybe he redesigns the cover of his company newsletter in a way you think is ugly and unsalable. Instead, the response from customers is overwhelmingly positive after the new issue goes out. "Sharp and eye-catching," one reader says. "Really attractive and easier to read," another writes. Such experiences teach you quickly to strangle your tongue and reserve judgment in situations where you once would have automatically screamed foul.

"You don't tell the other person anything," says Colleen Larson, who learned that rule after seeing her husband, Jerry, create a product she thought would be difficult to sell, but turned out to be a success. "It does not work for you to tell the other person. Let them learn it themselves." If your spouse asks your opinion, that's a different story. If not, think twice before giving your unsolicited two cents–you might be amazed what happens when your spouse approaches a situation from a different direction.

Jewelry designer Valerie Saint-Gaudens says her husband, Kenne Swink, is remarkable at discussing business matters–no matter how serious–with her without being mean or accusatory. It has taught her to be equally gentle in return. "When someone is that nice to you, how can you yell?" she asks. "Love takes over when I get flustered about something, and I give him the benefit of the doubt before I point out an error."

Seeing the real, rather than imagined, flaws in a spouse–and yourself–also can help strengthen ties. What better way to appreciate that you need each other than to have your shared business experiences illustrate–day in and day out–that she has an uncanny way of being good at the things you're not and vice versa? Simply put, it's that yin-yang principle that proves the two of you together achieve a balance, that in working together you can create something more powerful than either of you could alone.

For many work-at-home couples, it's almost uncanny how well one's knowledge and experience fills in the other's gaps in skill.

Colette and Ed Hoover have discovered their complementary backgrounds help them cover a wide range of client bases in their work as family business consultants. He was a veteran of the corporate world, while she had worked for years with non-profit organizations. Together, they can offer help and perspectives to many more businesses than either could alone.

Even couples in different businesses can do plenty to support each other's work. If he's an architect, for instance, and she's a public relations specialist, he might be able to offer design tips that will improve her newsletter, while she can review his bid proposals to make the writing and sales aspects shine.

Personality differences also can complement each other. If she's uncomfortable with people but has a knack for seeing the big picture clearly in any situation, and he's the ultimate schmoozer but tends to get lost in day-to-day details, she might want to take the lead in long-term planning while he handles responsibility for customer relations and marketing. Together, they can create a powerful venture that makes the best use of their talents. No matter how different your skills or endeavors are, you will find you can help each other tremendously.

Not that you should be content to allow your spouse to fill in for your weaknesses from here until eternity. The magic of running a business together is that you can be continually available to help, guide and teach each other–known in the corporate world as cross-training. Along the way, you also can acquire humility (when you're doing the learning) and patience (when you're the teacher).

And when it comes to work stresses and pressures, nothing's better for a home-based business person than knowing there's a warm, sympathetic shoulder and some encouraging words only a few feet away. We've found that, when one of us is feeling down about work, the other is likely to be stronger and more level-headed about the problems confronting us. A healthy Home Team has twice the emotional resources of a solo home-worker, so partners can pull each other up out of the trenches and boost each other over hurdles in a work-related crisis.

"It takes a skill in getting the other person moving along," James Patterson says. "Our valleys, fortunately, don't usually hit at the same time. You need to be able to encourage and push (each other)."

On the flip side, Home Teams in which spouses are controlling, jealous, abusive, bull-headed or fault-finding are in for trouble, both in their marriage and businesses. When you work together, the faults we all have plenty of are magnified. Whether spouses allow their differences to tear them apart or bring them together is their decision.

Working together as a Home Team is a wonderful opportunity to learn and grow–professionally, emotionally, spiritually, intellectually. One person alone in a home office can easily become isolated and stagnated if she isn't careful. But two people sharing home and work space? There are few better ways than a Home Team to prove that life is a continual learning experience. It might be frustrating at times, but it also can be wonderfully exciting–and excitement is a sure ingredient in keeping romance alive.

What other wonderful, romantic benefits await the Home Team? There's the sense of fun you can experience together, of being able to pop into each other's office for a second at almost any time to share a laugh over a comical typographical error in today's business section, or a silly joke a friend sent you online. There's the pleasure of reaping the fruits of your labor together–no, "He earns it, she spends it," routine in most Home Team households. There's the excitement of moving together toward the same goals, both in the family and in work. And there's the opportunity to enjoy real intimacy–not just the physical kind, but a closeness that comes from shared goals and dreams, shared experiences, and plain old shared time–something that's all too often a rarity in the outside work world.

And then, of course, there's plain old romance.

Your office or mine?

Imagine this: you realize one Thursday evening that the next day is the eighteenth anniversary of the day you and your spouse met. OK, it's not a landmark celebration like a silver wedding anniversary, but it would be fun–and a nice surprise for your spouse–to do something special on the occasion. Unfortunately, if you work in an outside office, it's too late to take the next day off from work–and it's certainly too late to come up with a plausible excuse that would convince your spouse to take off. You might be able to leave work early and meet her at her office after 5 p.m. to whisk her off on a romantic date, but you know how crowded all the nice places get on Friday evenings. So it's put up with the crowds or wait until Saturday.

If you're part of a Home Team, though, you have a third choice: sneak across the hall into her office at lunchtime the next day with a bottle of champagne, a picnic lunch delivered by a local caterer and a promise to shut off the phone for the next hour or two (making sure, of course, that she doesn't have any appointments or projects due that afternoon). You leave your offices, lower the bedroom blinds, tune in the radio to a soft music station, spread a picnic blanket on the bed and–voila!–instant romance.

OK, not every day will be like that for Home Teams. In fact, most won't. You're running a business like everyone else, and work needs to get done or you don't get paid. But plenty of opportunities are there when you want to take advantage of them. What a great way to enjoy a marriage and make the most of it–twenty-four hours a day, seven days a week.

"Romance is very important to us," jewelry designer Valerie Saint-Gaudens says. "I should think that even people with separate jobs would face the same challenge of keeping the romance alive. We try to have one date a week. Thursdays were our goal, but we don't hit it very often. Rather, we escape to a movie and dinner once in a while. I buy subscription tickets to the theater so we will be forced to go out to a nice dinner and a play every two months. Dressing up is very important! Get pretty! Flirt! Promise not to talk business over the merlot!"

Even with the fabulous advantages of the Home Team arrangement, romance doesn't just happen. If you want the best the lifestyle has to offer, you have to commit to planning, and seizing opportunities whenever you can.

"We keep our romance alive by taking the time to pay attention to each other," doll-maker Richard Creager says. "We take long walks together and discuss personal matters. We enjoy the outdoors. Romance is always there if you take time to pay attention to each other's needs. Whenever we can, we take a day off just to enjoy something together."

Sometimes, that day off can be extraordinarily special. Look at what photojournalist Bob Sherman arranged to enjoy with his wife, Carolyn: He chartered a Lear jet to New York, told Carolyn to wake up and get dressed, left their teen-age son a note stating they would be away for a while, and flew from their home in North Miami Beach to New

York City for a visit to the Carnegie Deli. One special meal later, they were back home–by one in the afternoon. People he told later didn't believe he did that–he had to show them the receipts to prove it.

It doesn't have to cost a penny to enjoy a workday date with your spouse, though. Creativity is more the key here. And a determination to make the most of the wonderful opportunities for togetherness the Home Team lifestyle gives you. After all, if you can't schedule personal time together, what's so special about working together at home?

"One has to work to kill romance–it's natural," cowboy-poet and author Ham Hamilton says. "I used to call Ellie on the phone and tell her to look at the sunset 'cause I couldn't be home to share it. Now, I find her and we go into the lawn and watch the sun disappear. We've been known to travel sixty miles to watch the sun come up over a particular mountain ... . Keep your arm outstretched and your lover will take your hand or snuggle to a hug–every time."

Romantic interludes

When should you take time off together? As often as you can. Why? For pretty much any reason you would like, but mostly just because you love each other and want to nurture that love. How do you make the time? You do what you have to, whether it's blocking out time on your calendars, arranging for a once-a-week baby-sitter or day-care class for your toddlers, buying theater subscriptions so you have to get out to see a play every few weeks, or just turning off the phones and locking the doors for an afternoon. The planning tips in the previous chapter should help in the cause. Spontaneity is needed in a relationship, but sometimes you will just have to plan to find the time in your busy lives.

And what do you do? Whatever you two enjoy. Here are some inexpensive suggestions, though:

- **The stroll.** No time just now for lingering dinners or overnight getaways? How about a simple walk in a scenic nearby park or forest preserve on a beautiful day? Just the two of you, hand-in-hand, strolling through the trees or past the pond on a weekday morning or early afternoon when everything's peaceful. No teens shooting hoops, no family reunion picnics, no hordes of joggers–they're all still in school or at the office. Ha, ha!
- **The special breakfast.** Get to bed early and wake up before sunrise (and children-rise) to enjoy a quiet breakfast for two on the patio. Brew some aromatic, flavored coffee, warm up some tasty pastries you bought the day before and relax together before the day's insanity begins.
- **The siesta.** There's nothing like an early afternoon nap, except perhaps an early afternoon nap preceded by another bedroom activity. You can stave off the afternoon blahs and have some privacy that will be lacking once the kids burst in from school.
- **The afternoon getaway.** You've been needing time together lately, but today the stress doesn't get to you because you've made plans to leave the office early together for a quiet 4 p.m. dinner. Your favorite restaurant is not crowded yet–in fact, you might have the place to yourself–and you will still get home in plenty of time to catch up on work ... or that romantic comedy on cable that starts at 8 p.m.
- **The day-long home date.** Has work been crazy lately? Pick a date when it looks as if things will be back under control, and plan to spend the day together doing ... whatever. Don't talk about work. Sleep in, buy chocolate-dipped strawberries to munch in bed, have your meals delivered, rent some movies and leave the blinds closed. If anything takes you back to the carefree days when you first started dating, this will do the trick.

Ten habits Home Teams can develop to ignite and maintain passion

We know you have developed common goals, dreams and interests. You certainly will remember to set aside time for dates and other relaxing time together each week. And, of course, you always will remember birthdays, anniversaries and other special dates, as well as commit to making those occasions extra special for your lover. They are important and should be commemorated, no matter how much your spouse might try to downplay them.

But you don't have to look weeks or months in advance on the calendar for ways to ignite and maintain passion in your Home Team relationship. When your spouse asks himself or herself the question, "Is my marriage partner a romantic, passionate lover and friend?" the answer won't be a reflection on the once-in-a-decade surprise trip to Hawaii, nor the car or flashy jewelry given years ago as a special gift. It will be in the little things you do every day. And, if you put your creative mind and a little extra effort toward it, you will come up with endless ways you can give your spouse the fun, romance and excitement that he or she needs and deserves. Do it unconditionally, but it's certain you will get that much and more in return.

A Home Team can ignite and maintain romance and passion with ...

1. Words. It doesn't take much effort to say kind, loving, sincere words throughout the day, and it can make all the difference in the world. Don't forget the three words every spouse wants and needs to hear at least every day: "I love you." "You're the best," runs a close second, and is especially important for men to hear. Make sure to let your spouse know that you think he or she is sexy–his arms, her legs, in his new shirt, in her new skirt.

Fooling Around

When you are running a home and business together, it's easy to find yourself talking about mistakes and differences throughout much of the day. While these areas do need to be talked through, set a policy to catch your spouse doing something right. When she lands a new client, when he comes up with an effective marketing campaign–anything major or minor that can bring praise–speak up and make a big deal of it. When someone hands you his or her work and asks, "What do you think?" the tendency is to point out everything you believe is wrong. That's how we've been trained. Instead, what's *right* about it?

Most of us have spent our careers in a corporate setting where we never got the praise we deserved for our hard work and top-quality performance. When you work at home, praise is going to come from a customer or spouse, or not at all. Customers deserve and expect high quality, and don't often go out of their way to praise, so the uplifting words need to come from the spouse.

Speaking frequently, honestly and deeply also can build intimacy. Make certain to tell your spouse your needs–don't make the mistaken assumption that she knows, or that, "If he loved me, he would know." When you're talking about any subject, watch your tone. Yelling and sarcasm are short-term fixes that produce long-term pain. Always strive to encourage and uplift.

2. Actions. While kind words are important, your spouse will watch to see what you are doing to back those words up. You've probably heard the phrase, "Marriage is a 50-50 partnership," many times in your life. That's wrong. A good marriage is a 100-100 partnership, with both spouses giving their all.

Doing more than your "fair share" will help bring you closer together. Don't keep score–"I did the dishes an extra day this week, so you owe me one"–it only leads to trouble and hurt feelings. Bust the mental Home Team scoreboard to pieces. Even if you think you're unfairly ahead, you end up losing. If you have free time, watch the kids when it's not your turn. Or lend a hand with product shipping. Make dinner. The scoreboard approach also tends to lead to a household cold war, in which the husband who feels his wife is not doing her share ends up cutting back on duties, she retaliates, and little positive gets accomplished from there and anger grows.

The act of forgiveness also will go a long way toward growing love. When you live and work together, you won't have an ounce of trouble finding something that can tick you off. Have patience, forgive, and love unconditionally. Don't hold grudges or make your spouse feel guilty about honest mistakes.

Many couples also report it turns them on when their spouses truly listen to them. It's easy to become preoccupied with business and household matters. If your wife tells you a flaming hedgehog has just scampered through the yard and set fire to the shed, and you find yourself saying, "Uhhhhh, huuuhhh," like Billy Bob Thornton in the movie *Slingblade*, perhaps you're not being as attentive as you should. Look your spouse in the eyes when she is talking. Think about what your spouse is saying before pondering what you will say next. Show interest in your spouse's interests.

Always aim to treat your spouse the way you want to be treated.

3. Touch. Couples who work together in the corporate setting know the unwritten rule: don't paw each other, or you risk making everyone in the office ill and becoming an ongoing joke around the office cooler. No such rule when it's just the two of you at home. Home Team spouses should strive to take advantage of the power of touch.

Fooling Around

While your spouse is busy at work and looking tense, stop by and massage her shoulders, or simply caress him on the arm. During breaks, engage in plenty of kisses and hugs. Each day, make at least one of each last for more than thirty seconds–a good, quick WOW! Hold hands whenever possible–even when you are having a disagreement. It reminds you not to say anything that will hurt the one you love. Give each other a full-fledged body massage at least once a week. Ahhhhhhhh.

4. Grooming. No, not the dog. You! One great benefit of working at home is the ability to wear whatever you want–sweat suits, underwear only, nothing. It's great to be cozy once in a while, but after a few weeks of wearing that favorite T-shirt every day it gets ... well ... disgusting.

Dress up in nice clothes for work every so often. It doesn't have to be an Armani suit, but put on an outfit that you could head out to dinner in. When you dress up, you feel better about yourself and have more confidence. But if you won't do it for yourself, do it for your spouse.

As a parallel to the clothes issue, it's easy to get up in the morning, read your e-mail, eat breakfast, head for the home office, work out and down lunch, back to work, dinner time, return for an hour to finish work for the night, and ... oh my gosh–it's 8 p.m. and I haven't showered!

Try to hit the shower and groom as early in the day as possible. Remember to spray on a nice fragrance, and have plenty of mouthwash on hand for those frequent kisses. Look, smell and feel great.

5. Fitness. Make exercise as much of your lifestyle as eating and bathing. It's not an option when time permits–it's mandatory. That gets you out of the New Year's resolution and after-letting-yourself-go exercise programs that almost always end up as disappointments. Work-at-homers don't tend to be the most active people in the world by nature of how they work, so if they don't compensate for that with exercise, there is going to be more of them to love.

Everyone should exercise regularly and eat well to develop short-term energy and long-term health. Most of us are never going to have the bodies we see on the late-night Tushersize infomercials, but we should do all we can to try to look our best for ourselves and our spouse. Exercise together if you want–it's a great way to develop a common interest and spend a few extra hours with each other a week. Drop those extra ten pounds (if it's healthy for you to do so) in coming months–it's guaranteed your spouse will respond in a romantic way.

6. Laughter. Studies in recent years finally have proven what some have claimed throughout history: there's incredible healing power in laughter. And it's a quality most people find sexy. Vow that you won't take life so seriously. If you, your spouse and the ones you love are reasonably happy and healthy, the rest doesn't really matter all that much. Have faith in your talents and enjoy the process on your way to success. The joy isn't at the end of the road–it should be found in everyday life. If you find yourself saying, "I'll have fun when ... ," or "I'll be happy when ... ," you will find yourself predominantly miserable and in for major disappointments. It's easy to forget to have fun as you struggle to build a better life for yourself and your family.

Pass each other funny comics in the office. Tell jokes. Watch funny shows or movies at least twice a week. Have a good time together while working and playing. No teasing about your spouse's "faults," however. Those slams may seem "funny ha-ha" at first but will boomerang as pain later.

Feeling depressed about work? Say you can't laugh? Spend an entire day in the office with giant antlers on your head. Go ahead–just try to feel miserable after that.

For many, there's nothing that's more of a turnoff than someone without a sense of humor. Not even someone with giant antlers on his head.

7. Flirting. Don't waste your energy flirting with the waiter or waitress at your favorite restaurant. Flirt with each other–there's a payoff involved. Include some sexy glances and winks in your workday. Brush up against each other. When your spouse is knee-deep in a project and on deadline, whisper in his ear that you have a reward for him at the end of the day, or project's finale. Respect that he needs to get his work done, but give him something to look forward to. Come up with fun sexual innuendoes ("I'd like to balance YOUR checkbook."). Forget to put on your underwear occasionally. Ooooops.

8. Surprise. Routine brings needed order to our lives, but too much of it makes life a bore. Consider your grooming habits: chances are good you shower, shave, brush your teeth, floss, comb and style your hair, apply deodorant and fragrance, and dress in a particular order, down to whether you put your socks on your right or left foot first.

Break routine. Aim to add the element of surprise to your lives. You don't have to hide and attack your spouse when he comes home, a la Cato from the *Pink Panther* movies. Strive for pleasant surprises. Even the most modern wives still love to find cards, fresh flowers or candies waiting for them. Buy each other small gifts for no reason. Leave sweet notes. When you're out–or if you're in a separate office down the hall–call for no reason other than to say, "I love you." Cook her breakfast. Bake him his favorite chocolate-chip cookies. Buy her that garden swing she's been talking about for years. Rent him time on a fishing boat. Try out a new massage technique. Make an effort to learn about her favorite hobby.

The cards and gifts on birthdays and anniversaries are expected. Strive to blindside your spouse with pleasant surprises. You know your spouse's likes and dislikes best–take those into account and be creative. We know someone who tends to buy his family members gifts they don't like much, but knows he can use them months down the road. Not fair! While it's nice to share a gift, make sure you also reward your spouse with surprises she alone can enjoy.

9. Attitude. A person's attitude can be a big factor in appeal. Your attitude might change through the years–perhaps without your noticing it–so step back and take an honest look at your attitude every so often. People tend to grow more cynical as they age, usually in response to frustrations about the sliders life throws them. And cynics tend to be lonely people.

Work to develop or reacquire a positive attitude. This topic is controversial–some say it's hogwash, while others claim it's the only way to live. Our take on it is that you should live life with a positive attitude, with a dose of reality to keep you in check. The cynic might say, "Why start a business? Most of them fail." A better way to look at it is to say, "You just might succeed–many have." The realism aspect is the commitment to do your homework and work hard. Positive thinking alone won't get you where you want to go–it must be coupled with prudent action. The positive thinker who does not act wisely ends up the fool.

Your attitude–the way you look at life and how you treat others–will affect both the way you view romance as well as what you get in return. Strive to be excited about all aspects of life, including work, marriage, parenting and play. Have a child-like approach to life in that you decide to find fun in everything you do. Be curious–explore new activities and interests. Perhaps you might not be up for skydiving, but trying a new type of cuisine is a good start.

10. Sex. While working as a Home Team provides great opportunities for great sex, entrepreneurship–especially when combined with parenting–can be exhausting. If you are not careful, sex can become as frequent as the change in seasons, or, just as bad, a let's-get-this-over-with-so-I-can-get-to-sleep service.

Frequent, exciting sex doesn't have to be just for newlyweds–it can be for any couple that commits to making the time for it, and strives to make the experience special. Sex is important–make it and keep it a priority, no matter how busy work and home life get. Besides being the most wonderful, satisfying activity the two of you can do together, it is the most intimate act between two people. Laziness or inactivity in the bedroom can snowball into an array of other frustrations and messy problems that will hurt your business and personal lives. Don't let that happen. Your spouse needs satisfaction, and it must come from you. If both spouses do their share, sex within the marriage can be better than most fantasies.

Let's start with the bedroom. Make sure your bedroom door has a lock–and use it. The bedroom should be a special place for the two of you–almost sacred–and that's why we are so adamant about the need to keep any sort of business out. No shop talk. No papers. No work done there. Ever. The lock also is needed to keep kids on the outside. If they are old enough to be unsupervised–or if another sibling can watch the youngsters–they have no business having full access to your bedroom at all times. It's none of their business what you're doing in there, whether it's playing gin or playing doctor. Click.

It might not sound romantic, but if you're having trouble finding time for sex, schedule it. No, not ten minutes, either. At least an hour. And no cancellations.

Other times, use sex as your getaway time when the mood strikes you both, and whisk your spouse away to the bedroom. Pressed for time? The office quickie can be wonderfully exciting.

Make sure you tell your spouse what you want and need sexually. Certainly don't take the "if he loved me, he would know" attitude into the bedroom–it will only lead to frustration. Communicate your sexual needs clearly.

Foreplay. Enough said.

Strive to add variety to your sex life. Scores of books have been written about the subject. Do you ever do anything new? Some find sex toys and food fun. Play games with each other–try naughty boss and secretary (switching places, of course). Come up with other creative roles. For us, role playing also tends to satisfy the need for laughter, as we have trouble taking anything of the like seriously and end up in stitches.

Speaking of stitches, have fun, but be careful. We're reminded of a real news story in the late 1980s, in which the man handcuffed his wife to the bedpost and put on a Spiderman outfit. Our Superhero got up on a chair and jumped toward the bed, but missed and hit his head on the dresser, knocking himself cold. The wife had no choice but to scream at the top of her lungs until someone sent help.

Ladies, wear exciting underwear to bed occasionally. Your husband wants to see you in it–and don't second-guess yourself, you look fabulous in it. Surprise him by sporting the latest fashion from Victoria's Secret. The purchase is sure to get the attention of the preoccupied man.

While most marriages tend to evolve from starry-eyed ecstasy into old-shoe comfort after a few years or decades, there's no reason you can't keep the stars shining no matter how overwhelming work becomes, how angry you might get at each other occasionally, or how aggravating the kids have been that day. It takes hard work–from both of you, not just one or the other. But ... the rewards. Meeeeeooooowww!

Fooling Around

Home Team Quiz 8: "Who Loves Ya, Baby?"

1) When was your last romantic date together?
   a) Come on. We stopped dating when we got married.
   b) We go out with friends for a nice dinner every once in a while.
   c) It was on our anniversary a few years ago–we took a really beautiful champagne cruise.
   d) We try to set aside special time for just the two of us at least a couple of times a month, but we enjoy romance every day.

2) How often do you tell each other, "I love you"?
   a) Never. We're married, remember?
   b) We don't have to. If we're married to each other, we already know we love each other, right?
   c) We always get each other mushy little love cards on our anniversary and on Valentine's Day.
   d) Oh, at least twenty times a day. Pretty much every chance we get.

3) What does your spouse wear when you go to bed together at night?
   a) I don't know. We sleep in separate rooms.
   b) Neck-to-ankle wool underwear–we don't have to look good when we sleep.
   c) He/she wore naughty underwear once, but it's usually sweats.
   d) Sometimes sweats. Sometimes a silky, skimpy slip (women only, please!) or fancy boxers (men, stick with these). Sometimes nothing at all.

The Home Team

4) Can you name the last day you two had sex?
   a) Day? I don't think I can even remember the year!
   b) Last month on the twelfth. That's our monthly day.
   c) About a week ago, I think. We would like more, but some interruption always seems to get in the way.
   d) Um, this morning after we were cleaning up the breakfast dishes. And yesterday morning. And Sunday afternoon while the kids went on a field trip. And ...

Score:

Did **a)** describe you? Don't believe those myths about marriage killing romance. Marriage should be the ultimate romantic gesture–not in that "happily ever after" fairy tale way, but in a way that celebrates a loving, lifelong bond.

Did you say **b)**? What's romantic about that? Make a point of enjoying special moments together–just the two of you–and truly showing and telling each other how much you care.

Was your choice **c)**? You're trying, but romance needs to be an every-day affair between the two of you, not a once-in-a-decade event.

Was **d)** the best match? Congratulations, lovebirds! Your approach toward romance is just right.

Chapter 9

Home Team Women
As Close as You Can Get to Having It All

Susan Detwiler remembers the moment that inspired her to leap from her job as a market research manager with a medical device company to self-employment as an information broker. With her second child on the way and "feeling like I was nine-and-a-half months pregnant," Detwiler put a critical eye to her work and discovered she didn't like what she saw. Office politics irritated her, and the direction of her career appeared uncertain. So she decided to research self-employment opportunities and found her niche in the field of health-care products.

Detwiler set up an out-of-home office when she started her business in 1985. She established her professional reputation and eventually began publishing the Detwiler Directory of Medical Market Sources, a nationally recognized guidebook in her field. But, even with new control over her career, the work arrangement had drawbacks. The main disadvantage: she was away from her children for up to ten hours a day.

So when she and her husband bought a larger home in Fort Wayne, Indiana, in 1993, Detwiler decided to make another move as well. The extra space allowed her to set up a home office, so she took a chance and did it. Despite her apprehensions, it took just weeks for her to admit she had done the right thing. "I'm rather enjoying working at home, and I didn't know I would," she says.

As with Detwiler, many women have discovered the special benefits of a home office. It takes them away from the stresses of the corporate world. It gives them the flexibility to have a balanced personal and professional life. It can even offer career opportunities that, in the work world, might be blocked by the "glass ceiling" and other subtle–or not so subtle–forms of discrimination against women. And, when they have a partner at home with them, the arrangement can be even sweeter.

Detwiler joined her husband, Mark, who already worked at home running a mail-order business that deals in collectible records. The arrangement has left both of them happier, she says. She starts work in the morning by popping into her office in an upstairs bedroom to check her electronic mail. While her computer downloads the newest messages, she heads downstairs to brew some coffee. "I'm much more relaxed," she says. She also feels better about being able to see her children–John and Ann–off to school and welcome them back in the afternoon: "I feel like I'm there for them. (Before), I was very much uptight about being at the office."

Corporate consternation

Many studies show women's frustration with the stereotypes of career success has skyrocketed since the 1980s. For women with children, "Supermom" clearly has proven to be an unrealistic goal. For married women without children, starting a family might mean a move off the corporate fast-track and into a dead-end or meaningless job that doesn't require overtime or travel. And, for many single women, career success might come at the expense of any kind of social life.

The stresses are showing.

In one recent study, more than half of the women surveyed said they would stop working if they had "enough money." In the late 1980s, just thirty-five percent gave that response. Mothers between the ages of twenty-five and thirty-four also say they are spending more time with their children, and bringing less work home from their offices.

In another survey, two-thirds of professional/managerial women and women business owners said they had changed their definition of "being successful" in the 1990s. They said success for them was determined more by relationships, self-fulfillment and spiritual values, and less by money and material things. An overwhelming majority–about seventy percent–of women also are saying it is important to have enough time for family and friends.

A more rewarding lifestyle

"One of the things that's great about working at home is that you feel like you can almost have it all," says Susan Fletcher, who writes novels for young adults from her Oregon home. Her husband, Jerry, is a former ad agency employee who works at home in a consulting and direct marketing business. "What a great thing, to do the work that I love and be able to spend time with my daughter," Susan says.

Being self-employed and working from home is probably the best way to satisfy both work and family needs, according to the Pratt study of home work. It reported that the majority of mothers and fathers who are sole proprietors have home-based businesses, and that only self-employment–presumably because the owner has control over the time and place of work–offers enough flexibility to make child care a possibility.

Not that women who work at home pull full-time double duty as moms and business operators. Most work around their children's schedules to some degree, or have someone–in or out of the home–watch their children while they work. The key is flexibility–knowing you can drop everything and be there immediately if Baby gets an earache, or that you can plan your workday around duty as chaperone on the sixth-grade field trip.

Women without children also reap plenty of benefits from the arrangement: "What I like about it is that I get to spend every day with Richard," says Jodi Creager, who with her husband crafts dolls at her Grass Valley, California, home. "He's the light of my life. This is the greatest joy I can possibly experience. I get to work with my best friend. I can't think of a better thing to do."

Having a spouse around who also happens to be a home business partner helps women in other ways. When a family responsibility arises–whether it is taking the ten-year-old to bassoon lessons or making an emergency run to the grocery store for milk–two people might be available for the job. The wife might handle most of the regular grocery shopping, as studies show most women do, but if she's on a tight deadline and he just finished his major project for the week, he probably will be able to take a break to go to the store.

Simply being in the home while working also can make life better for women: studies have shown home-based women like their work environment more than do women who work outside the house.

Valerie Saint-Gaudens, of Encinitas, California, certainly falls within that category. She says working at home creating custom jewelry with her husband, Kenne Swink, and being near their two children is wonderful: "I couldn't see living any other way, and would never consider working for anyone else."

Happier families

For mothers, being around to watch and help their children grow ranks as one of the biggest pluses: "My neighbor is a CEO, and she envies that I can work in a T-shirt and shorts and stay home with my baby while she had to go back at six weeks after her last baby," says Diane Pfeifer Justice, who writes humorous cookbooks. While Justice acknowledges her lifestyle can have more ups and downs than that of a well-placed and well-paid executive, it's a lifestyle she wouldn't want to give up.

Juggling work and children isn't easy. Many work-at-home women say it is their biggest challenge. Valerie Saint-Gaudens says there is "just no way" she could work from home with two children without help. The stress of trying to be businesswoman and mother was too much until she and her husband hired a live-in maid when her older daughter was about a year-and-a-half old. Since then, she's felt less pressure to be Ms. Everything. "Celine learned early on that I have a job–it's just not like other mothers who go off to work," she says. "She protested for a long time when she was a toddler, but the maid was able to distract her and let me work." On the other hand, Valerie adds, when her kids need her–or when she wants to enjoy time with them–she can be there in a flash.

Bob Sherman, of North Miami Beach, Florida, says he and his wife, Carolyn, started their home-based businesses for one reason–so she could be with their son as much as possible. In a previous marriage, Carolyn resumed working outside the home weeks after her daughter was born, and the girl grew up in day care.

"By the time she was two-and-a-half or three years old, she was calling the people in day care 'Mommy,' and not Carolyn," he recalls. "I told her there'd be no more of our kids calling other people 'Mommy' and not her." When their son, Roby, came along, that was no longer a reason for concern–Carolyn was working at home.

Mothers and non-mothers alike also enjoy other benefits from sharing both home and work with their partners. In many cases, husbands end up taking on a greater share of household responsibilities. This is especially true in business partnerships where wife and husband play equal roles. When that's the case, it often seems only fair that cleaning, cooking and other chores also are shared.

Michelle and Jim Foy of Winnetka, Illinois, reallocated household duties after they began working from home as management consultants. He took on the laundry in return for her handling household finances. In fact, he says he even enjoys cleaning and folding clothes, because it gives him time to think about work problems while stepping away from the office. Michelle says his foray into laundry duty–he also handles the vacuuming–broke down the chore barriers in their home. Besides, she adds, working and living with the same person is the best way to exist–job and home become part of the same, seamless fabric, and she and Jim make up equal parts: "That real sense of partnership–I love it."

Toby Myles and James Patterson have established a similar approach to home duties since they began working at home full time in 1992. The Olney, Maryland, couple–who run a graphic design and communications business–split most of the chores, although she cooks meals more often. Each is in charge of keeping certain rooms clean, and she handles the laundry while he takes care of the garbage and other outdoor duties.

They also take equal responsibility for their son, Corey. Each works four days a week and spends one day caring for Corey. A baby-sitter helps out three times a week, and Toby and James each work one evening to make up for the day spent watching their son.

Many of the possible benefits of working together are mutual–both husbands and wives should learn to respect each other's opinions and work. Both have to, if they want their home business and marriage to be successful. Even smart managers in the corporate office world are discovering the old, "I'm the boss and you do as I say," routine just doesn't work–it certainly doesn't stand a chance with a person you share both office and bed with. But for women–who historically have had little authority in family businesses and sometimes little say in their own families as well–the potential for equal footing and respect through a home-based business partnership is a plus that's hard to beat.

Susan Fletcher says of her husband: "I feel real fortunate that Jerry does respect my work. If I tell him 'I'm busy,' he will leave me alone. From a woman's standpoint, I feel lucky that he takes my work seriously."

Keeping expectations realistic

As wonderful as it can be to work from home, women need to remember it is not without challenges. That's especially true in homes with young children, who can place unmanageable burdens on any mother who tries to take on too much.

"I wasn't prepared for how difficult it was to work from home," says Colette Hoover, who with her husband, Ed, runs a consulting firm for family businesses. "Emotionally, it was a lot harder of an adjustment for me." The Hoovers worked from home for three years before moving into an office suite. Colette says the combination of work and family demands in the same space was often too much for her and her daughter. "It took a couple of years to lower my expectations in relationship to the house," Colette adds, "and to get my priorities straight about what it means to be a wife and a mother and a business partner."

While it's hard enough lowering expectations to accommodate dirty dish piles and overflowing laundry hampers, persuading a spouse to share those attitudes can be equally difficult.

"When you work at home, there are endless (chores) in the house," says Renata von Tscharner, who runs a public interest planning organization out of her Cambridge, Massachusetts, home with her husband, Ronald Lee Fleming. "You have to leave things dirty sometimes."

That solution, though, isn't always easy for her husband to swallow: "He grew up in a household where Mom didn't work," von Tscharner says. "There's a difference between a working mother and a wife who does nothing but household chores."

Fleming acknowledges having trouble accepting that sometimes: "Our work is collecting information, and there's a large amount of disorder in the office. When that also is translated upstairs to everyday life, it's hard on me psychologically."

While von Tscharner and Fleming have live-in help, most work-at-home couples must fend for themselves when it comes to housekeeping and child care. Many of these couples share household as well as work duties, but there still are plenty of partnerships where the split is nowhere close to 50-50. The Pratt survey of home-based business owners found that women working from home frequently encounter the same household burdens facing their corporate counterparts–women spend the equivalent of three business days a week on grocery shopping, cooking, cleaning, washing dishes and clothes, family paperwork and child care.

Trying to take on too many of these responsibilities in addition to running a business can be overwhelming. Jewelry designer Valerie Saint-Gaudens discovered that shortly after her first baby was born: "At first, I did all the housework and baby nursing, etc. About every six weeks, I'd have a breakdown and cry and cry over all the pressure, wailing that I wasn't Superwoman and just couldn't take it. My mother would come over during the days so I could work while she cared for the baby, but I was still stressed."

On top of that, their business wasn't producing as much income as they would have liked. Eventually, her husband took a full-time job outside the home. When that happened, they also decided to hire a live-in maid. Today, the business is thriving and Saint-Gaudens' husband is back home working full time–and the maid has stayed. "What a relief," Saint-Gaudens says. "I tell other women that I couldn't work at home without help. There's just no way to do both jobs."

There is another potential problem in trying to juggle too many jobs: guilt. Guilt that the house isn't as spotless as Grandma's used to be. Guilt that there are no more dress shirts for your husband to wear because the laundry has been put off for two weeks. Guilt that every minute spent working–even if it's at home–means one less minute of undivided attention for the kids.

Eloise McGraw remembers trying to deal with that last problem in the early years of her writing career, when she worked in her children's playroom. "It was just a matter of being available immediately," she says. Still, even being in the same room with her children didn't change the fact she was paying attention to something else besides them part of the time. "I think it was hard on the kids sometimes," she acknowledges.

Even with a caretaker to help out, the guilt doesn't always disappear, as Saint-Gaudens has discovered with her older daughter. "Celine, I fear, thinks I work too much," she says. "She complains that I don't play with her enough, and lays on the guilt. I continually strive to lessen my load to free time for them, and tell myself that she simply doesn't realize how lucky she is to have me here. One day she will."

That's the bright side mothers need to focus on when they are juggling a dozen jobs and battling guilt. Their children will grow up with the security of knowing where their mothers and fathers are, and having access to them when they need them. It doesn't hurt children to learn that parents have other responsibilities and interests besides them.

So, as a Home Team woman, be prepared for a few household hurdles, and try to deal with problems before they become insurmountable. It helps to lower your expectations about how often the bookshelves get dusted–your house won't make the cover of *The National Enquirer* for not living up to your mom's standards. It's also a good idea to delegate some duties so you're not expecting too much of yourself–depending on your circumstances, it could be something as simple as asking your partner to pitch in a little more with the dishes, or as drastic as hiring a live-in babysitter. Don't feel guilty if things at home aren't perfect. They never will be, no matter where you work or what you do. Enjoy the many advantages of working at home and being near your family, because no other workstyle can match it.

A more rewarding career

Just as it offers opportunities for a happier family life, working as a Home Team also can give women a shot at more self-confidence and satisfying careers. Many women, as Susan Detwiler did, are discovering they are sick of office politics, game playing and discrimination in the corporate world.

Proof of women's exodus from big companies for better opportunities is no further than today's news. Story after story describe how women are forming their own businesses to escape the hassles of the corporate world. Self-employed women who work at home with spouses can have it best of all. Not only do they enjoy all the other benefits of running their own businesses, they also have the best professional support around–someone who understands both them and their work, and has a strong interest in their success. That kind of backing is rare in even the best of corporations.

"I know I could never work for somebody else again," Susan Detwiler says. Colleen Larson says she feels much the same way. Before starting their sculpting business, she and her husband, Jerry, worked together at a Minnesota defense plant, where they met. Despite Jerry's companionship at work, Colleen was unhappy with her job: "I was a woman in a man's field. I didn't want to work there anymore."

Colleen worked at the plant for fifteen years before leaving in 1990 to sculpt full time. Now that she works for herself, the kind of inequities she perceived before no longer exist.

Saint-Gaudens says she, too, became disillusioned with the work world in the early years of her jewelry-designing efforts: "I worked at home for many years. This was great, but I lived with my mother, which made surviving easier. I later worked at jewelry stores, thinking the security would be nice, but the hours and lack of freedom turned me off. Then I dreamed of being an in-house jewelry designer ... because of the unlimited resources to produce my designs. I got my wish, but that turned into a nightmare when (a boss) went back on all his promises of royalties and promotions and simply cracked the whip."

Even something as simple as eliminating a long drive back and forth to an office every day can make life easier for women already struggling to make the most of each minute of their day: "For me, it's a great advantage not to have to commute to an office," planner Renata von Tscharner says. "I'm able to combine running a household and working. I can save the time of commuting."

Greater potential for success

By finding a more satisfying way to work and eliminating some of the corporate roadblocks, women also can improve their potential for higher earnings and career success. This isn't automatic, of course. Many home businesses can take years to become profitable–and some never do. And if a woman leaves a high-tech office career for a home-based business producing hand-made teddy bears, she might find it hard to earn anywhere close to what she once made. But, again, the potential for improvement is there.

Many women who work from home, though, say it's the less tangible career benefits that make it so appealing.

"I find I can get a lot more done," says Michelle Foy, a general management consultant from suburban Chicago. "I'm using my time in the best possible way." Bringing work and family together under the same roof can breed efficiency by combining the resources of an individual, a family and a business, making all three more effective. "There is a bleed-through, and we want it that way," she adds.

Vicki Palmquist says she and her husband, Steve, have discovered the same benefit in their desktop publishing business. The best reward of working from home, Vicki says, is the "tremendous increase in productivity. I get so much more done working in this office than in any other office."

The satisfaction alone of calling your own career shots is worth all the headaches and worries of leaving a wage position to take a risk on your own business, says Carol Kurtz, of Minneapolis. She and her partner, Steve Mudd, craft stained-glass art, and she says the experience is one she wouldn't trade for anything. "It's better to work together," Kurtz says, adding that her work is more rewarding than any job she has ever had. "It's so much nicer not having an idiot tell me what to do. It's very fulfilling."

Home career hurdles

Despite all the positives, women can face some tough career challenges in forming a Home Team. Escaping the inequities of a wage job doesn't mean women won't encounter discrimination in their own enterprises–the process of seeking loans, finding clients and establishing a professional reputation can be complicated by the double standards of the business world. Earnings also can suffer from the effects of discrimination.

On the plus side–although it's a sad comment on the way the business world sometimes operates–women who work from home with spouses are less likely to encounter these barriers than women in business for themselves. A man and woman together are much less likely to get the brush-off when trying to borrow funds from the local bank, or looking to sign up a male client who seems to be uncomfortable about working with female-run firms.

Although, historically, women have been more likely than men to start home day-care businesses or cottage industries, that is changing as women are leaving the corporate world with an increasingly broad experience in business, computers, finance and other specialized fields. Improvement also might come as women use their business savvy to raise what were once simple craft or cooking enterprises to big-time ventures with a nationwide presence. For example, consider Debbi Fields' success with her cookie baking experiment.

As women strive to make an impact in the work-at-home business world, they must recognize that motherhood can have a major impact on their careers. Many women, whether they choose to or simply have no alternative, put their business-building efforts into slow gear when they have youngsters.

Susan Fletcher, for example, says she didn't do nearly as much writing when her daughter Kelly was young. She chose to focus most of her attention on the baby. "It was very difficult, and I did not work full time at home," she recalls. "Kelly came out on top as being the most important thing I was doing." That meant working only during her daughter's naps and–later–for a few hours every week when Kelly entered preschool. "Once she started school, then I started having a more realistic schedule," Susan adds.

Maureen Carlson also altered her focus when her children were young. She stayed home from teaching after her daughters were born, and began sculpting for craft shows when her kids were one and two years old. When she worked, though, she made sure it did not interfere with caring for her daughters: "They were the priorities, and I did a lot of things at home," she says. "I really did work around what they were doing."

Even mothers who hire someone to help with household responsibilities might find their careers progress more slowly during their children's early years.

Ronald Fleming says his wife is less able to travel and meet other demands of their planning business because she spends more time on family matters, even with the support of an au pair: "It's harder for her to grow professionally because of the demands of working and being in charge of managing the household."

While women acknowledge that family responsibilities can limit their career progress, at least temporarily, most seem to accept it as a given in their lives. They agree that juggling roles can be difficult, but most don't express any regret for spending more time with their children and less time with their businesses for a few years. After all, having the flexibility to be with their families is the reason many of them started working at home in the first place.

Completing the circle

Women's careers have come almost full circle in the past forty years or so, from the stereotypical Donna Reed housewife of the '50s, to the driven corporate Supermoms in business suits and bow ties of the '70s and '80s, to the family-focused work-at-home women of the '90s and beyond. There are worlds of differences, though, between women who stayed at home a half-century ago because they had few other opportunities, and those who are staying home today because they want to and are able to create better all-around lives–personally and professionally–by doing so.

Unless we stop schooling girls after the eighth grade and take away women's voting rights, we'll never again see the day in which women will do nothing but care for families and homes. Yes, many married women work to help support their families, but it's more than that. It's that women, as do men, derive satisfaction from publishing that newsletter, creating that hand-made chair or closing that advertising deal.

Many women say they are happier if they have work beyond household and family–even if that means juggling a half-dozen roles and struggling to make sure there are enough hours in the day. A study by researchers at the University of California at Berkeley found that, of one hundred forty women observed in a twenty-two-year period, working women felt less disillusioned and less frustrated than full-time homemakers, and suffered from fewer chronic conditions.

While women have made progress in the job world, many are finding even better opportunities in home-based self-employment that can satisfy both their career and family needs. And, for the same reason, men are joining them at home in life and business partnerships ...

Home Team Quiz 9: "For Women Only"

What description best applies to you?
  a) I wish I had married a millionaire. At least then I could quit my job, hire a maid or nanny and watch soaps all day.
  b) I wish I had never gotten married or had kids. Then I could live life my way and focus on my career.
  c) I wish I had it all together more. I love being at home with my kids all day, but I want to express myself professionally, too.
  d) I wish I had it all together more. I love my career, but I want to be with my husband and kids more.

Score:
  Did you choose **a)**? Doing nothing isn't a lifestyle–it's a curse. Think about the skills and talents you have, then look at constructive ways to put them to use. Once you've done that, consider whether a Home Team would work for you.
  Was **b)** your choice? Don't live for your career–there's more to life. Think about the love that first brought you and your husband together, and that first inspired you to have children. If you can rediscover those joys, then you might want to think about forming a Home Team.
  Did you say **c)** or **d)**? A Home Team can offer just what you're looking for. Go for it!

Chapter 10

The Home Boys
Men at Work—and Play—in the Home

Gentlemen, welcome home.

If you are like most men, it isn't likely you have seen much of your house during daylight hours, so take a short tour with Gregory Real Estate. We're the two wearing bad blazers. Stand outside and admire the home for a moment. Nice, huh? That's one of your greatest expenses in life, one of the reasons you have been working so hard and gone so much.

While you are out there, glance skyward. See that bright ball of fire? (Don't look directly at it, silly.) It is commonly referred to as "the sun." Although the sun can do wonderful things such as illuminate and warm the earth, and remove the majority of clothing from people at the beach, it is powerless against the impenetrable barriers of workplace walls and cubicles. Although you might have had a suspicion during commutes that the world isn't always dark, and have some recollection of this from childhood, let this be your confirmation.

As we unlock the front door of your home and step aside to let you in first, you will see a female person, and perhaps some tiny people as well as creatures walking on four legs. Wait, Dad–don't run away! This is known as your "family." Wife–we present your husband. Kids, pets–Daddy. "Ahhhh," you say as you wipe your brow in relief. "They look so different when they are asleep."

Feel free to take a stroll inside the home if you feel the need to refresh yourself further. We'll just grab a seat off in the corner and talk about reasons why joining a Home Team can be the perfect way for men to live, as well as give tips on how men can get the most out of the arrangement.

Although the popular image painted of the American man has him spending his mornings at the yacht club, afternoons contemplating the color selection of his new Jaguar, and evenings sipping cognac in front of a roaring fire while reading books that will help him continue to rule the world, the truth is that most men today find themselves overworked, stressed, confused and distanced from their families. Man left home during the industrial boom and never really came back. He has become the absentee father–if not a divorced or, worse, "deadbeat" dad, then likely a sacrificial lamb slaving away at work for the "betterment of his family." He is often considered an economic tool above all else. He is thought of by society as a secondary parent. His image has taken a beating in the last three decades. Whereas father used to know best, television now portrays him as the buffoon. He is Al Bundy. Homer Simpson.

He will, on average, live a shorter life than his spouse. He is more likely to drop dead of a heart attack or stroke than his female counterparts. If disease doesn't do him in, his own hand might, as he is more than three times as likely than women to commit suicide: female suicides have declined thirty percent since the 1970s, while that number has risen eight percent for men, according to government statistics.

Yes, men continue to rule the high levels of the political and business arenas, and inequities in pay exist, but women and minorities are making inroads in these areas. With time and continued pressure, such discriminatory practices–we hope–will someday end. But the majority of the hard-working men in America are not living the good life.

They deserve better, and so do their families.

Most live every day with plenty of their own career frustrations, and are justified in how they feel. They might ...

- Find themselves stuck on the work treadmill with no apparent way off. Day after day, week after week, month after month, year after year;
- Not be recognized with adequate promotions, rewards and recognition for the high-quality work they are doing;
- Be sick of office politics as well as working for people they consider to have inferior talents;
- Fear today's unstable job world, as well as the trend toward making fewer employees handle more work;
- Talk themselves into believing they live to work, and that anything less is selfish;
- Work like a dog, yet never seem to make enough money;
- Do work they hate for the rest of their working lives because it pays "well";
- Be frustrated with the subsequent effect on ...

Family life

Whether Dad is beloved, despised or simply tolerated by the rest of the family, odds are he isn't around much, anyway. Forty percent of American children will lay their heads down to sleep tonight in a house where their biological father does not live. The effects are clear and staggering: seventy percent of long-term inmates and juveniles in reform institutions grew up without a father present. Even in stable, loving, two-parent families, Dad is all too frequently nowhere to be seen. He's off at work, putting in regular time, overtime, weekends, to bring home cash to improve his family's standard of living. Research shows dads today spend forty percent less time with their children than parents of the previous generation. The average father spends less than ten minutes–TEN MINUTES–a day with his child. He will spend more time on the toilet.

Fortunately, after being beaten over the head with evidence, America is starting to realize there's a correlation between the missing dad and some of society's biggest woes. A 1996 Gallup Poll found that seventy-nine percent of Americans believe "the most significant family or social problem facing America is the physical absence of the father from the home." That percentage shot up almost ten points in four years.

A divorce rate in excess of fifty percent as well as single parenting are both issues that play into this problem in a big way but are beyond the scope of the discussion here. We are assuming you both are hard-working, have a solid marriage and are committed to keeping it that way, and are loving parents. That already puts you in a small percentage of the population. But even given those wonderful qualities, men who follow the conventional methods of making a living are doomed to live separate lives from their families. There is no way around that.

Many a modern man finds himself groping for a happy medium between his responsibility as a substantial financial provider for his family, and a more active role as a spouse and parent. Some men are trying their best within the constraints, however. It is refreshing to see the efforts for a refocus on the family by men in recent years. While the most visible events–the Million Man March and Promise Keepers seminars—have been entwined with a dose of religious controversy, it's difficult to argue with the messages they are sending men about responsibility.

Some married men have even taken their parenting quest to the other extreme: they become stay-at-home dads. Whether based on who makes more money, or simply a family decision, more and more men are watching the kids while their wives head off to work. Nearly two million men a year are primary care providers for their children while their wives work, according to the U.S. Bureau of the Census. The concept, sadly, is considered radical. The Center for Research on Women in Wellesley, Massachusetts, found in a study of one thousand, five hundred CEOs that sixty-three percent said the reasonable amount of leave for a father to take after the birth of a child was "none."

Hogwash. Every father should take a break from work to spend time with his newborn. It should be as much a special time for Dad as it is for Mom. But the fact of the matter is, over the long haul, the nonworking stay-at-home dad concept is not realistic for most men. Few families can afford it, and, even if they can, most men cannot stomach the transition to strictly bread eater from bread-winner.

The complaints at-home dads cite over and over are isolation and discrimination. As is the case with the solo home worker, isolation often becomes unbearable with the wife gone and takes much of the joy out of the lifestyle. And while the idiotic "Mr. Mom" comments can be brushed off with a "funny ha-ha," what society says about a nonworking man is no laughing matter. Rather than being perceived as a loving, caring parent who is playing a major role in raising his child, he is looked upon more often as an unemployable failure.

Men need to work and are expected to work. It is a large part of what defines them. When someone meets a man at a party, the first question after the introduction is inevitably,

"So what do you do?" It's more than uncomfortable small talk–it's a way to place him in society. A five-year study of ten thousand men and women by Behavior and Brain Sciences found men in all cultures see beauty as the most important quality in a mate, while women base it on–you guessed it–a man's earning power and ambition. What response at that party would be more impressive: "I'm a cardiologist at the Mayo Clinic," or "I stay home with my son"? It doesn't matter if the doctor hasn't spent five minutes with his spouse or kids in the last three weeks, one response will elicit an "Oooooh," and the other will garner an, "Oh, that's ... um ... nice."

The other extreme, however, is where you find far too many other men who just can't get it into their heads that their physical presence in family life is vital. A colleague of ours spoke about his mentor at work, who is approaching age fifty and recently had been married for a third time. The mentor's first two wives couldn't deal with the long hours he worked away from home to establish his business, nor his neglect of the homefront, and the marriages fell to pieces as the couples spent little time together. Have we learned our lesson this time? He tells our colleague over a few beers: "If I can continue to make the living I'm making and hang onto this wife, I will be a happy man." Sky-high goals at the office, low goals at home.

Make no mistake: no matter where a man works, he can have a satisfying family life if he makes it a priority. However, for the man looking for the best balance between a career and family, there is no option with more potential than to form a Home Team.

Modern home work is "a way to involve fathers in the lives of their kids in a way that hasn't happened since the industrial revolution," says Dr. Wade Horn, who works from his Gaithersburg, Maryland, home. Horn is a child psychologist and family expert who is president of the National

Fatherhood Initiative, a group aiming to promote the need for fathers to play a greater role in their kids' lives.

"Culture has sent a message that, as long as (men) are good bread-winners or send their child support, they have fulfilled their responsibility and the children will be just fine, thank you," Horn says. "We disagree. Although that is important, being a good father is more important than being a bread-winner.

"You look at the decline of the status of children in America and find a significant correlation with the number of children growing up without involved and committed fathers. If you hope to improve the well-being of the children, you have to do something about the increase in father absences."

The National Fatherhood Initiative outlines three essential ingredients to manhood and fatherhood: time, commitment and responsibility. Let us take a look at these and see how they can be applied to the Home Team arrangement:

• **Time.** The concept of "quality time" that was popular during the 1970s and 1980s is finally starting to be exposed as the joke it is. It doesn't matter, the thought goes, if you spend five minutes a day paying attention to your spouse or child, as long as it is a "quality" five minutes. There simply is no such thing as quality *minutes*. Men must spend both meaningful AND plain-old *quantity* time with their wives and kids if they hope to develop deeper relationships, and help their children grow.

A Home Team brings the entire family back together under one roof. Not pieces of the puzzle. Everyone. And the man is the piece that, for years, was lost under the couch with the dust bunnies. A Home Team can put men back in the picture for an extra eight, ten, twelve or more hours a day. Home work can be a gift to men, a tremendous chunk of time that once might have appeared written off for good. It fulfills the quantity end and, if men schedule and prioritize properly, it gives them more opportunities for one-on-

one or family time together for everything from projects to play.
- **Commitment.** A man must be committed both to the marriage and to his children. We have spoken at length about the absolute need for commitment to the marriage if the Home Team lifestyle is to succeed and be enjoyed. Remember, it takes work, but the payoffs are enormous. The same holds true for parenting. As the fatherhood group reminds men, resumes and golf scores are not read at funerals. Attendees will talk about what kind of husbands, fathers and friends the deceased were. Men must keep that in mind when planning both work and free time.
- **Responsibility.** Any major decision a father makes, the group says, must be stacked up against how it affects his child's well-being. Regardless of which spouse works where and makes how much money, one of a father's primary responsibilities is to ensure his kids are well-fed, safely housed, healthy and clothed.

As part of a Home Team, a man can play a more active daily role in helping ensure his family's needs are met. From a financial standpoint, while there are risks to any business, the potential also is there for a man to help boost his family's standard of living. With proper planning and by taking calculated risks, his chances of success in a home business are greatly increased.

The pleasures–small and large– for the man at home

Horn spent most of his life in the traditional workforce before his work with the National Fatherhood Initiative, which allows him to do many of his duties from home and spend time with his daughters, who are now teenagers. While he certainly needs quiet work time–especially when giving phone-in media interviews on behalf of the group–he says he enjoys the increased communication with his kids throughout the day the most.

"There is little difference in work productivity between taking fifteen minutes off to chit-chat with co-workers here and there than to spend an extra fifteen minutes with the kids," Horn says. "Yet, that fifteen minutes with the kids will go much further than with co-workers."

His greater household presence also has placed him at home at key times, such as when one of his daughters was battered as a pre-teen. Horn says an older boy at the bus stop picked her up, threw her in the mud and kicked her. When she came flying through the door in tears, Horn was there to comfort her and deal with the matter–which would not have had the same effect if he had to do so over the phone from a workplace. In this instance, working at home allowed him to fulfill his parenthood role of comforter and protector. "I don't care if I was on a call-in show with Dan Rather," Horn says. "I would have hung up that phone the minute I saw her come through the door, covered in mud."

The extra ten to twelve hours a week of "unproductive, frustrating time" Horn used to waste commuting in the Washington, D.C.-area traffic now can be put to better use, such as the afternoon he brought the family guinea pig to school for his daughter and watched her present it to the class.

Bob Sherman has been running home businesses with his wife, Carolyn, for more than two decades. Their son, Roby, was three when they started a photojournalism business and later added an information brokerage at their North Miami Beach, Florida, home. "It has been a tremendous pleasure to know, as (Roby) was growing up, that he wasn't a latch-key kid," Bob says. "I had the wonderful opportunity to spend many, many hours watching my child grow up.

"I got to see more of him than other people see of their children," Bob adds. "The average working father comes home at 6 or 6:30, the family eats dinner, and the kids are off to bed. I was here when he came home from school at 3. Yes, I was busy at times, but at least I got to see him. It was a pleasure I would not have had if I worked out of the house."

There will be those who will question the masculinity of the work-at-home lifestyle: "Help with the chores? Help with the kids? Spend more time with the ball-and-chain?" Absolutely. In fact, it gives men the opportunity to exemplify what manhood should be about–chasing a lifelong dream; becoming best friends with his spouse; being a more involved parent in aspects ranging from play to discipline; showing kids firsthand that a man should treat his wife with love and respect, as boys will learn how to relate to women by watching their fathers interact with Mom, while girls will discover this way what they can expect from men; teaching kids values, including faith, commitment to a solid work ethic and enjoyment of life.

Ten keys to success for the work-at-home man

When men we interviewed talked about problem areas resulting from working at home, or wives pointed out concerns, the challenges usually fell into one of the following ten areas. Even if the men could not pinpoint what the problems were, the challenges usually could have been solved by paying greater attention to one or more of the following keys:

1. He must deal with perceptions well. Let's face it: society says a man's place is not in the home. It is in the office. While a work-at-home man won't take the abuse of the longtime nonworking Dad, he certainly must fight the fight personally and publicly about how the world views him.

While this problem is nothing like it was a decade ago, it is still present. The work-at-home man must first convince himself that he is doing the right thing, then he can move on to proving it to others.

The harshest critics often are members of your own family. But before you whip out the verbal bazooka, look at it from their perspective for a moment. Maybe Mom and Dad worked hard to put you through college and saw the rewards in your nice job and fancy title downtown. It is a big jump for them to hear about your decision to leave all of that to start a business at home, a concept the odds are good they cannot relate to in the least. Explain to them and the wisecracking siblings what you are doing, but save your energies and keep the faith. Chances are, the only thing that will prove you right is time.

Friends come a close second on the list. Scott still has friends who call at 4 p.m. and ask if he just got up and what was on *Jerry Springer* today (the answer, of course, is crossdressing cultists). While the pals are kidding, it also is clear from conversations that some of them have no idea why or how a man would work at home. Again, you won't convince people overnight.

Have fun with those who don't or won't get it. Ham Hamilton, a sixty-year-old poet and author from Chubbuck, Idaho, sure does: "My neighbors somehow thought I was retired for the first year. Some now think I'm retired, but have a great hobby. I have always been a practical joker, so I added fuel to the stories. My clergy knows the truth, has a good sense of humor, and doesn't blow the cover."

It is normal to have moments of doubt. As you sit at your computer in the morning with your bed-head reflection in the monitor looking back at you, and glance out the window to see a slick neighbor wearing his thousand-dollar suit drive by on his way downtown, there will be times you will ask, "Am I doing the right thing?" or "Am I less successful?" But, if you are doing the work you love and sharing life with your family, you know the answer deep inside. Take pride in what you are doing. Don't put on a different face because of what anyone expects. Never apologize about this. Ever. As Ralph Waldo Emerson said: "Whoso would be a man must be a nonconformist."

2. He must yank the plug on work. The workaholic syndrome can rear its ugly head even in the home, and for some men it can be worse than it was in the workplace. The top complaint of work-at-home men is, "The work is always here. I can't get away from it." You can and you must. Yes, a home business takes a lot of effort–especially in the early stages–and there are days in which overtime is required to meet deadlines. But don't make a habit of working from the moment you awaken to an hour before you hit the hay. Otherwise, there is no point in living this lifestyle. Walk away and shut the office door at a reasonable hour, and leave the business thoughts behind with the papers.

Overworking at home often is an extension of the male martyr syndrome. You must believe that it is your right to enjoy life beyond work.

3. He must define himself properly. Men who end up saying things such as, "My work is my life," are in for the same disappointments as women who take on the philosophy, "My kids are my life." All aspects of life are important, but keep them in balance. If you don't, when the work falters, everything goes down the drain with it. One of the big reasons men take on this attitude is because of the economic expectations society has placed on them. A man's work is important to him, and it fulfills an important ingredient in manhood, but he should never be solely defined by his work, or by how much money he makes.

4. He must not neglect male bonding. As Scott looks out his window during the workday, ninety-nine times out of a hundred, it looks as if the Fathership came and swept away all the men on the earth while he was busy pounding away at his PowerBook. Plenty of kids and mothers, but not a man to be seen. Did he miss a meeting about this? Did all the guys get a free ride to the Planet of Perpetual Sports? Shucks, he should have watched the news last night.

As most men continue to work traditional jobs, it is sometimes easy for the work-at-home man to feel he is the last male on earth. Gone are the office basketball tournament pools, daily arguments about whether the Cubs will ever win another game, much less a pennant, and copies of the latest sick cartoon. Sure, these things aren't life or death in the grand scheme, but it's all part of bonding that men crave.

Men certainly need women–and, as we have said, we certainly hope a man's wife, not his dog or drinking buddy, is his best friend. But men also need men. And, too often, it is easy for this aspect to get neglected–especially by Home Team couples who find themselves saying, "We do everything together."

It is wonderful to share a wide range of experiences with your spouse and kids. But, once in a while, men need to go off and be with "the guys." We are not talking about "get in touch with your manhood" expeditions to the woods in which they eat off the land and communicate with burps. But a football game outing, men's club at church, game of pickup basketball, or trip to a favorite watering hole–whatever your pleasure–here and there is needed.

Just as it is easy for men to lose touch with other guys when they work at home, women also can contribute to the problem. Women, please don't give your man a hard time about spending an occasional evening with friends if he is working hard at home, and being an attentive husband and father. And men must remember to return the favor to their wives.

5. He must have his own space and private time. Just as man needs time with friends, he needs time to himself. And when you work and live in the same place, private time can be hard to come by.

Men, make sure you insist on occasional solitude. The best place to accomplish this is somewhere outside of the home office. There is too much to distract you there. A spare bedroom can be wonderful, but anywhere with a door and outside of the family traffic path will do. Men need to get away and think. And, we hope, pray. Without this time, it is easy to become robotic. No TV, no radio. Silence.

The family schedule will make this effort impossible at certain points of the day, so this must be planned. Late at night and early in the morning are great times for solitude. These help you reflect on the previous day and contemplate the day ahead.

Throughout the workday, the bathroom can be a quick ten- or fifteen-minute retreat—just make certain there is another bathroom available for the rest of the family, or you will find yourself constantly shouting, "In a MINUTE." You also can make the garage or basement your cave for longer getaways.

Along with physical space, men also need mental distance. When spouses grow closer and husbands are communicating well, women sometimes exuberantly push the matter too far with frequent, "What are you thinking?"-type queries. Whether out of concern or simply a quest for greater intimacy, this can become a bit much.

Let's use Scott as an example. At some points when he is quiet, Scott might be thinking about the ramifications of NAFTA. Other times, though, he's contemplating something such as, oh, how much water he can hold in his mouth, or whether he can jump up and reach that store awning. Or, remarkably, he doesn't have a single thought going through his head. He's just taking a mental vacation to Jamaica. Whatever the case, he shouldn't need to share all of his thoughts. There is a difference between not communicating and not communicating everything. And, speaking of which ...

6. He must communicate well. This came up so often it bears repeating here in the men's chapter. While men do need their space, they also tend to bottle things up, so it is easy to understand why wives are often concerned about their thoughts. Men usually are not very good at making eye contact, so they miss most of the nonverbal (and, too often, verbal) communication women send their way.

Clear, loving communication is something most men need to work on. It is important that they make the effort to get better. Women, give your man time. If communication has been a problem for years, you can't expect him to let his thoughts and feelings flow like the Mississippi River once he starts working at home. A man can start by making a conscious effort to look at his wife when she is talking, and by repeating what she said in his head as if there will be a test on it later. He also must work at letting his wife regularly know his thoughts and concerns.

7. He must fight competitive urges. This is a tough one for most guys. They are raised to be competitive in school, sports and everything they do. In adulthood, the workplace usually provides the outlet for men to compete. When a man works at home, he might find himself competing with his wife.

While a little competition can be healthy–some couples say it spurs them on to greater things in business–a lot spells trouble and hard feelings, and the loser just might take his or her ball and go back to the traditional workplace. Men must watch that they are not working against their spouses. Use the competitive spirit to reach goals in business and life plans. This also will keep a man from getting complacent. Men, if you still can't get competition out of your system, go out and play basketball or some other sport once a week.

Also remember, men: give credit to your wife when credit is due. If you work together, it is "our" business instead of "my" business. Emphasize the partnership aspect when dealing with people.

We have seen stories of some work-at-home men who lost their minds because their wives made more money than they did one year. Who cares? This is completely silly. Remember the "team" in Home Team. Encourage and edify each other.

8. He must let go. The work-at-home man must realize he cannot control everything. There is only one thing in life he can control, and that is himself. He certainly must not control his spouse through words and actions. The work-at-home woman must not suffer the same discrimination at home that she might face in the workplace. The marriage must be a partnership of equals, not of superior and subordinate.

Man also must admit that he cannot control all aspects of the world. While a woman's body reminds her of this monthly, this is often a tough admission for the man to make. Regardless of his abilities, man is going to fail at times, and this fact can be jarring. Sickness, injury and age can have the same effect. Man cannot beat himself up or stew over what is beyond his reach.

9. He must fight impatience. If a man is new to work-at-home life, it will take both him and his family time to adjust to the changes. This is especially true when it comes to the kids. If the man's attitude comes off as, "Dad's here and he's taking over," he will have a rebellion on his hands. Before offering a ton of ideas on how to "improve family operations," sit back and watch how everyone interacts. Be patient–give the arrangement time to work. And give your businesses time to succeed. Think long term.

10. He must fight perspiration. That is, not sweating the small stuff, which most of it is. Work hard, but have fun. Enjoy the lifestyle. Men deserve it as much as women.

Well, men, you and your family have some catching up to do. Welcome back. We'll just grab our blazers and see ourselves out.

Home Team Quiz 10: "For Men Only"

What description best applies to you?
 a) I wish I would win the lottery. At least then I could quit my job, get my wife off my back about money concerns and spend my life at the golf course.
 b) I wish being married and having a family didn't take so much time and energy. Then I could live life my way and focus on my career.
 c) I wish I had a better, more-rewarding job. Everything else in my life–home, wife, kids–is great, but my work is nothing but a wasted nine hours a day to earn money.
 d) I wish I didn't have to be away at the office so much. I love my career, but I want to be with my wife and kids more.

Score:
 Did you answer **a)**? Doing nothing isn't a lifestyle–it's a curse. Think about the skills and talents you have, then look at constructive ways to put them to use. Once you've done that, consider whether a Home Team would work for you.
 Did **b)** best match your feelings? Don't live for your career–there's more to life. Think about the love that first brought you and your wife together, and that first inspired you to have a family. If you can rediscover those joys, then you might want to think about forming a Home Team.
 Was your choice **c)** or **d)**? A Home Team can offer just what you're looking for. Go for it!

Chapter 11

Root, Root, Root for the Home Team

Why *wouldn't* someone want to join the Home Team trend? Think of all the pluses of a successful Home Team: freedom, companionship, self-determination, and a fuller, more integrated life–for *everyone* in the family. You get to share fun and work, and lifelong dreams with your partner. You can be there in an instant when your kids need you. Your kids can gain security, comfort and a life-influencing education–maybe even some work experience and cash. There's something in it for everybody–if you are determined to make it work. It won't happen without a serious and loving commitment–from both of you.

Is it always easy? Of course not. Neither is running a triathlon, writing a great novel or inventing a better mousetrap–but people who do these things gain tremendous rewards and personal satisfaction ... and can even have plenty of fun along the way. You can, too. You will feel more in control of your career. You can have a richer homelife. You can make far better use of your time than do most people who have to struggle with daily commutes, office politics and other energy drains. You will even be kinder to the environment, whether it's by cutting back in the number of miles you drive every day or by indirectly reducing the demand for office complexes.

Once you have decided to make the Home Team lifestyle your own, you will need a plan for success–just as Iron Man competitors have to train for years, novelists have to block out plots and flesh out characters, and mousetrap makers have to design blueprints. Every couple will develop their plans differently, but the points we've covered in this book should help guide you no matter what your situation.

Believe in yourselves

Home Team partners can get so much out of their lives and work, but it takes faith. First, you need to believe in what you are doing–we hope the two of you are chasing your dreams together, and you have decided that becoming a Home Team is the best way to catch those dreams. This is a lifestyle you should be *excited* about entering–because it's one that can help you achieve personal and professional satisfaction far beyond that enjoyed by most people. No punching someone else's time clock or "ball-and-chain" spouses here.

Second, you need to believe there is no time better than now to start your Home Team, or at least to begin planning. These are thrilling days for entrepreneurs and home-based business people. Technological advances that allow small-business owners to compete with mammoth, traditional corporations–high-speed modems, cellular phones, fax-on-demand, personal digital assistants, interactive Websites, etc.–keep coming so fast, you are likely to miss a few dozen if you don't pick up a newspaper or go online for a day or two.

It's also a great time for marriages–people are figuring out that commitment means something, that multiple divorces and no-strings-attached relationships are damaging to individuals, families and society. Call it what you want–a return to family values, cocooning, a reality check–the result is the same: a desire for a richer and more meaningful life. What better way to celebrate these two trends–in business and in relationships–than by bringing them together as a Home Team?

Each of you needs to believe in each other as much as in yourself. There's no getting around the team aspect of this lifestyle. But what great things you can accomplish. Both of you will grow in ways you might never have predicted, and you can become wiser and better people because of it. Women, you can avoid falling into the traps of the "little woman" stuck at home without professional rewards while raising children, or of the duty-juggling, corporate mom who's exhausted by stress. Men, you will discover you can earn a solid living and have a great homelife ... one that matters to you, your spouse and your kids. And neither of you will have to fear the home office as a place of exile–unlike people who work from home alone, you're never far from a second opinion, a pat on the back or a shared laugh.

To make the most of the Home Team lifestyle, it's best to share as many goals as you can. If you have separate enterprises but are eager to share office space, equipment and expertise, that's great. If one of you has decided to start a new business and the other is committed to helping wherever he or she can, that's even better. Best of all, though, is if you can share the same business as a team–you're not necessarily doing the same work or developing the same skills, but each of you complements the other and plays one part of a greater whole. The synergy you can develop in this arrangement is incredible. Whichever approach you choose, though, give it all you've got. A Home Team is not for the half-hearted, either in work or your relationship.

Passage to a new world

Here's the most important point to remember as you get started: this is a new lifestyle that will take some settling into. You might not always feel comfortable with the arrangement to begin with, and you will encounter surprises along the way. What will get you through this transitional phase and keep you on the right course is a commitment to making your Home Team work.

Think of it as the marathon-runner's wall: there's a point along the race when a runner might feel on the verge of collapse, that there's just no way she will be able to put her right foot in front of her left for one more step. Every part of her body is screaming to stop–NOW. And then? She passes through that wall. The screaming stops, the feet keep moving and she finishes the race.

Now, your Home Team wall–actually, there will be plenty of walls along the way–might not be as all-encompassing or traumatic. If you've prepared well, those moments might be simply disorienting, frustrating or discouraging. Keep working your way through them, though, and one day you'll have your "eureka" moment–when you realize you've slipped completely and comfortably into the lifestyle of the home-based entrepreneurial couple. It will finally feel right–and it will feel better than any lifestyle you have known.

A few things have to happen first, though. You need to be professionally and financially prepared for any business you choose to launch. Make sure you have studied as much as possible, lined up appropriate financing and developed a realistic business plan before that first day in your new home office.

Next, you have to prepare psychologically. That's where the lessons we've outlined come into play. Are the two of you ready to work together? Do you really want to? You both must be sure you can cooperate in a joint venture without big-time clashes over every small decision. Think back to past projects you have worked on together. Were you able to honestly but gently express your opinions while shopping for a bedroom set? Did you reach a decision on which church to join–yours or his–without hard feelings? Have you been able to negotiate family holiday visit schedules that satisfy you both? If you can say yes to such questions, you have a good foundation for the Home Team lifestyle. If not, you might want to hold off and first work on improving your communication and other relationship skills, because both you and your spouse are entitled to an open, warm and supportive working atmosphere. You should be able to expect better things from each other than you have ever expected from anyone else in a workplace. The marriage always comes before the business.

Remember that working as a team doesn't require you to surrender your individuality. In fact, it's a learning experience that can help you become better individuals. It requires you to hone the skills of kind but effective negotiation, solid but flexible planning, and straightforward but respectful communication. It will challenge you more than any other office environment, but the results can be wonderful. As with anything else in life, the more you challenge yourself, the more you grow.

In getting ready to work together, you will also need to sit down and make sure you are on the same track about all the other things that will be affected by your new home/office arrangement. Who will do what in the business and in the home? How will other family responsibilities–children, pets, aging parents and so on–fit into the mix? Where do you hope to be in five years? Ten? Thirty? These and similar decisions need to be made as you develop your Home Team life plan. You don't have to set them in stone. In fact, you shouldn't, because flexibility is key to both a successful business and a successful relationship. But you should agree on your guidelines and be ready to follow them as needed. That's both the benefit and challenge of being your own bosses: you get to set your own rules.

Having a road map to guide you along the way is important, because the Home Team lifestyle is different from any other workstyle. You will hear uncomprehending remarks from friends and family, you might feel disconnected, overwhelmed or just uncertain about what to expect next. So laying a proper foundation is vital–if you have a firm reason for doing this, if you are committed to this and have a clear idea of how to reach your goals, you will find it easier to overcome the obstacles popping up in front of you along the way. You will be better equipped to deal with those, "Oh, they're unemployed," comments, those non-stop requests for help with odd jobs "since you're not really busy," those constant telephone interruptions and your own impatience if you don't seem to be progressing toward your goals as quickly as you would like. You will be able to keep an open mind, stay patient, and always keep your eyes on your Home Team mission: to work well together, to be successful at what you do, and to have fun doing it.

What, where and how?

As the two of you forge ahead, you might need to assume new roles, or at least adjust the ones you already occupy. Knowing exactly who does what in a two-person team is vital for the success of your business and the health of your marriage. We're not talking a boss-employee relationship, though. Your roles are best established through your individual skills, interests and limitations–and they are best decided through communication and mutual agreement. And if your skills, interests and limitations change over time, then so, too, will your roles.

Once you have decided who handles which duties, take care not to step on each other's toes. Of course, you can offer helpful opinions and gentle–not critical–suggestions, but you should honor each other's primary responsibilities. It's an everyday show of respect that will help nurture both your homelife and worklife.

Communication and compromise are keys to Home Team success. Understanding each other–your individual ways of dealing with people, responsibilities and challenges–and giving each other space to do your own thing is the best way to coax the fullest potential out of the marriage and your shared enterprises. From there, you can focus on what really matters: working toward your personal and professional goals ... together. And the top goal always should be to make the most of your relationship. Don't let work overwhelm you. Always make sure you have time to yourself and with your family. Because, without love, rest and a healthy personal life, even a multi-million-dollar-a-year business will leave you feeling empty and dissatisfied.

The ultimate goal

That's where the greatest rewards of a Home Team lie: in making the most of your lives together. The more you work together, spend time together and pursue common goals, the richer your marriage can be. You can get to know each other more intimately–rather than grow apart–as time goes by. You will have to grapple with more issues than couples who spend their days apart in separate jobs, separate duties, separate lives. You will be tackling business plans as well as retirement plans, office equipment purchases as well as family room furniture purchases, client negotiations as well as negotiations over your kids' curfews. All these responsibilities might take time and energy, but they will also pay wonderful dividends: you will have so much more to talk about, so many more rewards—business and personal—you can reap together, so many more reasons to keep moving forward through life in the same direction. Those are true blessings in a marriage. In fact, that's what marriage should be all about, but far too often isn't. The divorce rate in excess of fifty percent is clear evidence of that.

Fast-forward now to a point in the future when you are ready to retire—or maybe just slow down a little in your business (some never want to stop doing the work they love). What do you want to do together then? Sell your business and devote your time to volunteering and grandparenting? Start a new, less-demanding business enterprise? Move to a warm, sunny climate and take up golf? Whatever it is, imagine how much better prepared you will be if you have been spending time together and sharing responsibilities all those years beforehand. Successful Home Teams don't expect that retirement surprise of so many other couples: "Hmmm, we haven't spent more than three consecutive waking hours alone together regularly in more than thirty years—what do we do now? What do we have in common anymore? What do we talk about?" Home Teams can spend the bulk of their lives together discovering answers to those types of questions. And, if they have done it right, they will like the answers.

Women, how much more meaningful could your relationship be if you and your husband didn't spend most of your married lives in separate compartments—he at the office and you at home with the kids, or maybe you in a different office and the kids in day care? As rewarding as full-time parenting can be, one day your kids will be grown and out of the house ... and it will be just you and your spouse again. It's a great comfort to know at that point that you share interests and actually want to—and can—spend time together.

Men, how much more satisfying could your lives be if you didn't feel tied to the stereotyped role of bread-winner above all else? Wouldn't it be great to share–rather than simply hear about second-hand–some of those landmark moments in your children's lives: the first step, the first word, the first day at school? Wouldn't it be wonderful to have the opportunity, day in and day out, to stay best friends with the woman you fell in love with so long ago? Home Team men have the opportunity to play a role in the family far beyond the caricature of distant disciplinarian and money-earner. Yes, it's more responsibility, but it's also the best way to make sure you grow close–and stay close–to everyone in your family, now and into the future.

And what could be more romantic than directing your lives together, deciding when you want to take time off, get away on a sunny day, or slip under the covers on a rainy afternoon when you need to escape the office for an hour or two? Only Home Teams regularly can enjoy those kinds of advantages, those intimate moments that help keep a marriage strong over a lifetime. What wouldn't you give for that kind of relationship? Isn't that worth the work it takes to make a successful Home Team? We certainly think so, and so do millions of other couples who are working together successfully.

Go to it, you two

So how do you get started? If the two of you have dreamed for some time of starting your own business, sit down and talk about how you can begin, who would do what, and when you will be able to get your home office rolling. Spend time researching your field, saving up for the big day and looking forward to your coming venture. Read and reread this book–and make use of the many other resources we've listed in Recommended Reading–to anticipate what sort of changes you can be in for, and where you want this lifestyle to take you.

If you are working as a Home Team, maybe you will want to re-examine some aspects of your arrangement. There might be challenges you could handle differently, responsibilities you could divide in a more satisfying manner or goals you could set that would make you both happier. Or maybe you're on the right track but just need more steam to keep moving–perhaps some household help, a regular vacation, more romance or a reorganized office setup that helps you maximize your effectiveness.

And if you're a Home Team that's been trotting forward successfully for some time now–congratulations. You've achieved something wonderful and admirable, and you both should know it. But what about the future? Have you mapped out the coming ten, twenty or thirty years together? If you haven't, you should. If it's been awhile since you have, now's the time to sit down together and talk about your long-term goals and dreams. People's interests, skills and desires change over time, and you might be surprised at some of the turns your partner's aspirations have taken since you last asked.

Make a point of talking regularly about your ideal future, to make sure the two of you keep moving ahead in a direction that satisfies you both. A Home Team, after all, is more than a five- or ten-year plan–it's a lifelong commitment that involves every aspect of your lives together. Do everything you can to ensure that commitment stays a strong and happy one. Because there's no other workstyle like it–no other arrangement that can offer such great rewards.

There is no doubt–the best possible team for two people in love is the one that allows them to spend time and chase dreams together, and share both personal and professional responsibilities. It's the one that can nurture intimacy, build strong relationships and help keep spouses moving forward in the same direction throughout their lives. It's a Home

Team, of course. Do it right, and you two are going to love it. We're rooting for you.

Afterword

Every Home Team will encounter moments of apprehension: Will I be able to work at home with my spouse? Can we run the same business together? Will we be able to share an office? Will cash flow allow us to pay our bills this month? Will anyone ever break down and do the laundry?

This book was one of our moments. An extended one. And it was a biggie.

We each have written thousands of newspaper and magazine articles in our lives, so that has become second nature. We also have worked together on plenty of projects in our home businesses. We don't always agree, but we talk things out, so that aspect is no sweat anymore.

But what we had not done is write a book. And, despite a newspaper clip file that we could set ablaze and warm Fargo with for a month or so, we had never written anything more extensive than a grocery list together.

We are mild-mannered compared to many in the writing business. But writers tend to defend their work like no profession you have ever seen. It is never business. It is always personal. Most writers part with words as easily as a Rottweiler parts with a rump roast. You don't meet many jolly, healthy old newspaper and book editors, and we writers are to blame.

The monster was sporting two heads:

One was shouting that we would never write a book after we had talked about it for so many years. Staring ominously at us as we write this is a yellowing copy of a 1984 *Writer's Market*, a book we have purchased every year since, hoping to come up with ideas and motivation to overcome our fears and write our first books.

The other head was laughing hysterically that we would end up maiming each other over "creative differences" while trying to write a book about how to work together. The head was bobbing and singing, "Isn't it ironic, don't you think? A little toooooooo ... ."

The ensuing years have been as easy as fishing with a fork. The challenges we faced are enough to fill another book. We shall spare you the gory details.

But in the end, the idea to mesh our writing didn't do us in. It saved us. In fact, it is doubtful that either of us alone would have finished this book. And even if one of us had, it certainly would not have been as complete. Each of us went through prolonged slumps. And, every time, the other was there to pick up the writing slack and keep encouraging until we both were on track again. Together, we got the job done.

We are proud of this book, and we certainly hope you learned some tips that will make your marriages, lives and businesses better, and had a little fun along the way.

Despite what the world says, you can have a great marriage and live life more under your terms if you work hard and play hard together, and are committed to each other. It is not always easy to be a Home Team, but it certainly is worth it.

We're off to drop the final manuscript in the mail now, and after we do, we have a bottle of chilled celebratory champagne waiting for us, and a thirteen-year-old *Writer's Market* that has a date with the backyard fire pit.

We look forward to hearing your Home Team stories. May your special marriages and lives, and your businesses be blessed.

Best always,
Scott and Shirley

Recommended Reading

Business/Marketing:

Employ Your PC: Businesses That Can be Run From Home, Gabriele Massie (1996, Red Tail Publishing)

Guerrilla Marketing: Secrets for Making Big Profits from Your Small Business, Jay Conrad Levinson (1984, Houghton Mifflin Co.)

Homemade Money, Barbara Brabec (Betterway Books)

How to Build a Successful One-Person Business, Veltisezar B. Bautista (1995, Bookhaus Publishers)

How to Raise a Family and a Career Under One Roof: A Parent's Guide to Home Business, Lisa M. Roberts (1997, Bookhaven Press)

In Love and In Business: How Entrepreneurial Couples are Changing the Rules of Business and Marriage, Sharon Nelton (1986, John Wiley & Sons Inc.)

Marketing Without Megabucks: How to Sell Anything on a Shoestring, Shel Horowitz (1993, Simon & Schuster)

Visionary Business: An Entrepreneur's Guide to Success, Marc Allen (1995, New World Library)

Working from Home: Everything You Need to Know About Living and Working Under the Same Roof, Paul and Sarah Edwards (1994, Tarcher/Putnam)

Working Solo: The Real Guide to Freedom & Financial Success with Your Own Business, Terry Lonier (1994, Portico Press)

Parenting:

Kids Are Worth It! Giving Your Child the Gift of Inner Discipline, Barbara Coloroso (1994, Somerville House Publishing)

The Parents' Resource Almanac, Beth DeFrancis (1994, Bob Adams Inc.)

Raising Confident Kids, Robert G. Barnes (1992, Zondervan Publishing House)

Relationships/Romance:

101 Nights of Grrreat Sex, Laura Corn (1995, Park Avenue Publishers)

Bridges to a Passionate Partnership: A Realistic Approach For Couples Who Want to Become Better Friends and Lovers, David LeClaire (1996, Hara Publishing Group/Equestrian Press)

Recommended Reading

Marriage Can Be Fun, Jon K. Kardatzke, M.D. (1995, New Wings)

Rock-Solid Marriage: Building a Permanent Relationship in a Throw-Away World, Robert and Rosemary Barnes (1993, Word Publishing)

Other helpful books:

Father Facts 2, Wade Horn (National Fatherhood Initiative)

How to Win Friends and Influence People, Dale Carnegie (Pocket Books)

The Magic of Thinking Big, David J. Schwartz (Prentice-Hall Inc.)

Megatrends for Women: From Liberation to Leadership, Patricia Aburdene and John Naisbitt (1992, Fawcett Columbine)

Myths and Realities of Working at Home: Characteristics of Home-Based Business Owners and Telecommuters, Joanne H. Pratt (U.S. Small Business Administration)

Not Guilty: The Case in Defense of Men, David Thomas (1993, William Morrow & Co.)

Magazines/Newsletters:

Entrepreneur, Published monthly by Entrepreneur Media Inc., (800) 274-6229, www.entrepreneurmag.com

Home Business News, Published quarterly by the American Home Business Association, (801) 273-5450, www.homebusiness.com

Home Office Computing, Published monthly by Scholastic Inc., (800) 288-7812, www.smalloffice.com

The Home Team™ newsletter, Published every two months by Panda Publishing, (888) 447-2632, www.bookhome.com

Income Opportunities, Published monthly by IO Publications Inc., www.incomeops.com/online

Organizations:

American Association of Home-Based Businesses Inc., Beverly Williams, President, P.O. Box 10023, Rockville, Maryland 20849, Phone: (800) 447-9710, (301) 963-9153, Fax: (301) 963-7042, Website: www.aahbb.org

American Home Business Association, Sam Burggraaf, President and CEO, 4505 S. Wasatch Blvd., Salt Lake City, Utah 84124, Phone: (800) 664-2422, (801) 273-5450, Fax: (801) 273-5422, Website: www.homebusiness.com

Home Executives National Networking Association (HENNA), Laura M. Vaughn, Executive Director, P.O. Box 6223, Bloomingdale, IL 60108-6223, Phone: (630) 307-7130, Fax: (630) 307-7140

245

Home Office Association of America, Richard Ekstrakt, Chairman, 909 Third Ave., Suite 990, New York, NY 10002-4731, Phone: (800) 809-4622, (212) 980-4622, Website: www.hoaa.com/

International Association of Home-Based Businesses, P.O. Box 4841442, Denver, CO 80248-1442, Phone: (800) 414-2422 (800-41-IAHBB), Fax: (303) 425-9675, Website: www.chejauk.com/iahbb/iahbb.htm

International Homeworkers Association, 1925 Pine Avenue, Suite 9035, Niagara Falls, NY 14301, Phone: (716) 284-6387, (716) 284-6402, Fax: (905) 572-6164, Website: www.homeworkers.org/

National Association of Home-Based Businesses, Rudolph Lewis, President, 10451 Mill Run Circle, Suite 400, Owings Mills, MD 21117, Phone: (410) 363-3698, Website: www.usahomebusiness.com

National Association for the Self-Employed, Bennie Thayer, President, P. O. Box 34116, Washington, D.C. 34116, Phone: (800) 232-6273, (202) 466-2100, Website: www.nase.org

National Federation of Independent Business, Jack Faris, President, 53 Century Blvd., Suite 300, Nashville, TN 37214, Phone: (800) NFIB-NOW, (615) 872-5300

(For information on other organizations in your area, contact your local or state chamber of commerce or small business development center. Or call SCORE–the Service Corps of Retired Executives, a resource partner of the U.S. Small Business Administration–at (800) 634-0245.)

Resources for Women:

American Business Women's Association, 9100 Ward Parkway, P. O. Box 8728, Kansas City, Missouri 64114-0728, Phone: (816) 361-6621, Fax: (816) 361-4991, Website: www.abwahq.org

Formerly Employed Mothers At the Leading Edge (F.E.M.A.L.E.), P.O. Box 31, Elmhurst, IL 60126, Phone: (630) 941-3553, Online address: femaleofc@aol.com

Home-Based Working Moms, P.O. Box 500164, Austin, TX 78750, Website: www.hbwm.com

Mothers' Home Business Network, P. O. Box 423, East Meadow, NY 11554, Phone: (516) 997-7394), Website: www.pleiadesnet.com/org/MHBN.1.html

National Association of Female Executives, Website: www.nafe.com

Recommended Reading

National Association of Women Business Owners, 1100 Wayne Ave., Suite 830, Silver Spring, Maryland 20910, Phone: (301) 608-2590, Fax: (301) 608-2596, Website: www.nawbo.org

Resources for Men:

At Home Dad, Website: www.familyinternet.com/dad/dad.htm

Fatherhood Project, James A. Levine, Director, c/o Families and Work Institute, 330 7th Ave., 14th Floor, New York, New York 10001, Phone: (212) 268-4846, Fax: (212) 465-8637, Website: www.fatherhoodproject.org/

National Fatherhood Initiative, Dr. Wade F. Horn, Director, 600 Eden Road, Lancaster, Pennsylvania 17601, Phone: (717) 581-8860, Fax: (717) 581-8862, Website: www.register.com/father/

National Home-Based Business Virtual Center of University of Wisconsin/Whitewater, Website: www.wisbus.uww.edu/homepg/home.htm

Parents at Home, Website: www.iquest.com/~jsm/moms/

Small Business Advancement National Center, Website: www.sbaer.uca.edu

U. S. Small Business Administration, Phone: (800) 8-ASK-SBA, Website: www.sbaonline.sba.gov/

Other Helpful Resources:

America Online, "Ma 'zine," Keyword: moms online

CompuServe, Working at Home Forum, Keyword: go work

Home Office Computing/Small Business Computing, Website: www.smalloffice.com

247

Index

Aburdene, Patricia and John Naisbitt, 26
Adin, Richard and Carolyn Edlund, 107
Allen, Gracie and George Burns, 90
Amway, 41
Au pairs, 145

Baker, John and Gail, 129
Ball, Jeff and Liz, 99
Barbeau, Brad and Rosemarie, 118-119
Burns, George and Gracie Allen, 90
Business plan, 73-74, 75

Caller ID, 128
Carlson, Dan and Maureen, 46-47, 71-72, 91, 98, 103, 157, 208
Censor, Alex and Meera, 112-113, 160-161
Center for Research on Women, 216
Child care,
    And Home Teams, 140-146
    In home, 143-146
    Out of home, 142-143
Children,
    And child care, 140-146
    And Home Teams, 136-153, 168
    Guidelines for, 147-151
    Using work to teach, 54, 137-138
Communication,
    And time management, 168
    Home Team benefits to, 60
    Importance of, 95, 96, 102-105, 236
Compatibility, 64-66
Copreneurs, 26, 28
Creager, Richard and Jodi, 80, 96-97, 181, 198

Criscenzo, Jeeni (and Joe), 83, 85, 93, 106, 176
Cross-training, 178-179

Desgrosseilliers, Michael and Marjorie, 40, 58-59, 160
Detwiler, Mark and Susan, 38-39, 116, 123, 129, 139, 147-148, 149, 162, 195-196, 204, 205
Differences,
    Resolving, 93-94, 106-108
Distractions,
    Managing, 84-86, 122-130, 132
Dorfman, Julie and Jerry Herst, 138

Edlund, Carolyn and Richard Adin, 105, 107
Emerson, Ralph Waldo, 223
Exercise/diet,
    Importance of, 130-132, 187-188

Family,
    And Home Teams, 140-146
    And conventional work, 31-33, 47-48, 136
Fatherhood,
    And stay-at-home dads, 216-217
    Challenges, 213, 214-217
    Gallup Poll, 215
Fields, Debbi, 207
Flaxenburg, Eric and Jean, 92, 137
Fleming, Ronald Lee and Renata von Tscharner, 58, 96, 113, 137-138, 155, 162, 202, 208
Fletcher, Jerry and Susan, 84, 114, 120, 124, 139, 156, 158, 197, 201, 208
Flexibility,
    Importance of, 79
    To set own schedule, 54-55

Index

Flirting, 189
Foy, Jim and Michelle, 47, 49, 53, 72-73, 81, 96, 120, 147, 154, 200, 206
Frey, Carlos and Sherian, 85, 126, 131, 148-149

"Glass ceiling," 196
Goals,
  And family plan, 40
  Defining, 38, 94-99, 232

Hamilton, Ham and Ellie, 96, 98, 182, 222
Hanson, Bob and Margaret, 86, 108, 126, 170, 176
Herst, Jerry and Julie Dorfman, 138
Home office,
  Adjustments to, 81-84
  And comfort, 57-58, 169-170
  And organization, 112-118
  And privacy, 129-130
  And socializing, 159-163
  And technology, 35, 231
Home Team,
  And child care, 140-146
  And children, 54, 136-153
  And companionship, 46-47
  And home-field advantage, 25
  And romance, 173-194
  And society's perceptions, 79-81, 84-86, 125-127, 221-222
  As a learning experience, 58-59, 176-179
  Benefits of, 23-24, 25, 28, 29, 34, 45-63, 230-231, 236-238
  Challenges, 106-108, 112-135
  Commitment, 66-70, 94-95, 231-232
  Compatibility, 64-66
  Definition of, 23
  Getting started, 70-73, 233-236, 238
  Quizzes, 43-44, 62-63, 88-89, 110-111, 134-135, 152-153, 171-172, 193-194, 211, 229
  Types of, 24-25, 35-42
Home workers,
  And career satisfaction, 26-27
  Growth in number of, 27
Hoover, Ed and Colette, 47, 51-52, 64-65, 82, 97, 104, 106, 178, 201-202
Horn, Wade Dr., 217-220
Housekeeping,
  And hired help, 121-122
  Challenges, 119-122, 202-203

IDC/Link,
  And estimated number of home workers, 27
Income Opportunities,
  Survey of home workers, 26

Justice, Jeff and Diane Pfeifer Justice, 108, 199

Kurtz, Carol and Steve Mudd, 156-157, 206

Larson, Jerry and Colleen, 87, 91, 114, 121, 126, 155, 177, 205
Laughter,
  Importance of, 188-189
Life plan, 73-74, 75-78, 234-235
Loneliness,
  And solo home businesses, 29
Love, 50-51, 61, 173-194
Lutnes, Keith and Jo, 95, 129, 136

Marriage,
  And business, 26, 97
  And Home Teams, 68, 231-232
Massachusetts Mutual Life Insurance Company, 26
McGraw, Bill and Eloise, 203
"Me" generation, 42
Megatrends for Women, 26

249

Men,
  And communication, 226
  And competition, 226-227
  And control, 227-228
  And families, 213, 214-230
  And Home Team benefits, 212-229, 237-238
  And keys to Home Team success, 221-228
  And male bonding, 224-225
  And overwork, 223
  And privacy, 225-226
  And stress, 213-214
Million Man March, 215
Mom-and-pop shop, 29-31
Motherhood,
  And Home Teams, 141-142, 197-200, 201-204, 208-209
Motivation,
  And goals, 98-99
  And mutual support, 179
Mudd, Steve and Carol Kurtz, 156-157, 206
Myles, Toby and James Patterson, 51, 85, 131, 161, 175, 200-201
Myths and Realities of Working at Home (see Pratt report)

Naisbitt, John (and Patricia Aburdene), 26
Nannies, 145
National Fatherhood Initiative, 217-220
Office (see Home office)
Organizing,
  And time management, 167
  Conflicts involving, 112-119
  Professional help with, 115-119
  Solutions, 115-118

Palmquist, Steve and Vicki, 73, 125, 126, 158, 206
Patterson, James and Toby Myles, 51, 85, 131, 161, 175, 179, 200-201
Personal appearance,
  Importance of, 187-188
Pets, 123-124
Pettingell, Bob and Charlene, 108
Pfeifer Justice, Diane and Jeff Justice, 108
Plan, business, 73-74, 75
Plan, life, 73-74, 75-79, 234-235
Poulos, Thalia, 115-118, 130
Pratt, Joanne, 27
Pratt report (*Myths and Realities of Working at Home*), 27-28, 197-198, 202-203
Priorities,
  In life and work, 49-50, 77
  Marriage as top priority, 97
Privacy, 129-130
Promise Keepers, 215

"Quality time," 218-219

Relaxation,
  And Home Teams, 60, 154-172
  Options, 163-165
  Tools for, 166-169
Respect,
  Importance of, 67, 69
Risks,
  And conventional business, 26, 28
  And home-based business, 26, 38, 39, 76
Roles,
  Defining, 90-94, 235-236
  Importance of, 91-92
Romance,
  Actions that build, 185-186
  And attitude, 190
  And communication, 184-185
  And Home Team lifestyle, 61, 173-194
  And sex, 61, 191-192
  And surprise, 189-190

Index

Importance of, 173-194
Options, 182-183
Requirements for, 184-192

"Safety zone,"
And space conflicts, 115-116
Saint-Exupery, Antoine de, 42
Saint-Gaudens, Valerie and Kenne Swink, 36-38, 83, 92, 98, 114-115, 139, 159, 169, 177, 181, 198-199, 203, 204, 205
Schandel, Terry and Susan, 34, 105, 115, 161
Sex,
And Home Team lifestyle, 61, 191-192
Sherman, Bob and Carolyn, 119, 139, 154, 181-182, 199-200, 220-221
Shtull-Trauring, Aron and Simcha, 72, 102, 104-105
Socializing,
Importance of, 159-163
Options for, 162-163
Solo home businesses,
And loneliness, 29
Stress,
And work, 29, 70
"Supermom," 141, 196
Swink, Kenne and Valerie Saint-Gaudens, 36-38, 83, 92, 98, 114-115, 139, 177, 197-198

Taxes,
Deduction benefits, 56
Technology,
And home office, 35
And time, 31
Telecommuting, 41-42
Telephone,
And time management, 128-129, 166-167
Time,
And technology, 31

Timeout,
In resolving conflicts, 103-104
Tinsley-Wickes, Nina and Robert Timothy Wickes, 161
Touch,
Importance of, 186-187

Understanding,
Between men and women, 100-105
Importance of, 99-108
Yourself, 101
Your partner, 102
United States Bureau of the Census, 216
United States Small Business Administration, 27

Vacations,
Importance of, 156-157
Planning for, 157-159, 165
von Tscharner, Renata and Ronald Lee Fleming, 58, 87, 96, 113, 137-138, 202, 206

"We" generation, 42
Wickes, Robert Timothy and Nina Tinsley-Wickes, 161
Women,
And Home Team benefits, 195-211, 237
And career challenges, 207-209
And career satisfaction, 209-210
And stress, 141, 196-197
Work,
And stress, 70
Conventional work and family, 31-33, 47-48, 137
Working at home,
And relaxation, 154-172
And security, 52-53
Financial benefits, 55-57
Trend, 25-27

251

Send now for your free copy of *The Home Team*™ newsletter

As thanks for purchasing this book, you are entitled to a free copy of *The Home Team*™ work-at-home newsletter. Each bimonthly edition is packed with expert information that will help you in your quest to make your work-at-home lives more enjoyable and your businesses more profitable, and we make sure you have a few smiles, to boot. Our expert columnists offer advice on an array of vital subjects ranging from marriage issues, to working as couples, to parenting, to marketing.

Our columnists include (as of publication):

• Scott and Shirley Gregory, newsletter editors, speakers and authors of *The Home Team: How Couples Can Make a Life and a Living by Working at Home*.

• Dr. Robert Barnes, marriage and family therapist, and author of many marriage and parenting books, including *Rock-Solid Marriage* and *Ready for Responsibility: How to Equip Your Children for Work and Marriage*.

• Jay Conrad Levinson, author of the internationally acclaimed, best-selling *Guerrilla Marketing* series of books, and co-founder of Guerrilla Marketing Int'l.

• Lisa M. Roberts, mother of four, business owner and author of *How to Raise a Family and a Career Under One Roof: A Parent's Guide to Home Business*.

See the Order Form to subscribe. For your free sample, send:

• Your name, address, phone and e-mail address, with a self-addressed, business-sized, stamped envelope (55 cents) to:

The Home Team newsletter
P.O. Box 3834
Naperville, IL 60567-3834

All information must be included. No phone calls for free issue, please. Columnists are subject to change. Please allow 2 to 8 weeks for delivery, depending on where we are in the publication cycle.

National Work at Home With Your Spouse Day
The Home Team M.V.P. Awards
January 16

January 16 each year has been designated as a national day of celebration for all couples who work at home. Whether it's a full day of fun or something as simple as a dinner out, we encourage all spouses to break from work and do something special in celebration of the lifestyle.

As part of the day's festivities, we will be awarding: The Home Team M.V.P. (Most Valuable Partner) Awards. Write in 1,000 or fewer words why your spouse deserves to be recognized for the award in this calendar year. Five winners will receive a one-year subscription (or extension) to *The Home Team*™ newsletter. One of those five will be picked as the Grand Prize Winner and additionally will receive a gift basket valued in excess of $100.

The deadline for the contest is Dec. 1 of each year. The easiest way for you to enter is by visiting our website (www.bookhome.com), where you also will find additional contest rules. You also can send your entry to The Home Team M.V.P., P.O. Box 3834, Naperville, IL 60567-3834. If you want a list of rules or winners mailed to you, send a self-addressed, stamped envelope to that address.

Winners will be posted on the website each Jan. 16, as well as featured in *The Home Team*™ newsletter. Happy celebrating, and good luck!

Order Form

- If you would like copies of *The Home Team* for yourself or for a work-at-home friend, or would like to subscribe to *The Home Team*™ newsletter, the fastest and simplest way is to call Panda Publishing toll free during business hours at:

1-888-447-2632
1-888-44PANDA

Please have your Visa or MasterCard handy. Orders only at this number, please. Direct questions to 630-357-3196. Your satisfaction is guaranteed.

- You can find out more information about *The Home Team* book and newsletter, or place your order quickly and safely 24 hours a day by visiting our website:

http://www.bookhome.com

- You also can order at your convenience by completing the form below and faxing it to us at: 630-357-3197.
- Or you can order by mail by copying or removing this form and sending it with a check or credit card information to: Panda Publishing, P.O. Box 3834, Naperville, IL 60567-3834.

Please send me ___ copies of *The Home Team* at $22.95 each.

I also would like ___ subscriptions to a full year of *The Home Team*™ newsletter at only $49.

Name: _____

Address: _____

City/State/Zip: _____

Telephone: _____
E-mail: _____

Shipping: $4 for first book via Air Mail, $3 for each additional book. No charge for newsletter shipping.

Illinois residents, please add 6.75 % sales tax.

Credit card number: _____
Type of card: _____ Expiration date: ___/___
Name on card: _____

Signature: _____

Care to Share Your Work-at-Home Stories?

What have been your greatest moments in working at home together? What have been your biggest challenges, and how did you resolve them? If you have stories or advice of any sort to share that might be of help or interest to other work-at-home couples, we would love to hear them. The Gregorys might use the stories in ensuing editions of *The Home Team* or other books. Visit the Panda Publishing website (www.bookhome.com), or send them to the Gregorys at P.O. Box 3834, Naperville, IL 60567-3834.

Order Form

- If you would like copies of *The Home Team* for yourself or for a work-at-home friend, or would like to subscribe to *The Home Team*™ newsletter, the fastest and simplest way is to call Panda Publishing toll free during business hours at:

1-888-447-2632
1-888-44PANDA

Please have your Visa or MasterCard handy. Orders only at this number, please. Direct questions to 630-357-3196. Your satisfaction is guaranteed.

- You can find out more information about *The Home Team* book and newsletter, or place your order quickly and safely 24 hours a day by visiting our website:

http://www.bookhome.com

- You also can order at your convenience by completing the form below and faxing it to us at: 630-357-3197.
- Or you can order by mail by copying or removing this form and sending it with a check or credit card information to: Panda Publishing, P.O. Box 3834, Naperville, IL 60567-3834.

Please send me ___ copies of *The Home Team* at $22.95 each.

I also would like ___ subscriptions to a full year of *The Home Team*™ newsletter at only $49.

Name: _____

Address: _____

City/State/Zip: _____

Telephone: _____
E-mail: _____

Shipping: $4 for first book via Air Mail, $3 for each additional book. No charge for newsletter shipping.

Illinois residents, please add 6.75 % sales tax.

Credit card number: _____
Type of card: _____ Expiration date: __/__
Name on card: _____

Signature: _____